The Life and Times of Elijah

BIBLE STUDY GUIDE

From the Bible-teaching ministry of

Charles R. Swindoll

INSIGHT FOR LIVING

Charles R. Swindoll is a graduate of Dallas Theological Seminary and has served as senior pastor of the First Evangelical Free Church of Fullerton, California, since 1971. Chuck's radio program, "Insight for Living," began in 1979. In addition to his church and radio ministries, Chuck enjoys writing. He has authored numerous books and booklets on a variety of subjects.

Based on the outlines and transcripts of Chuck's sermons, the study guide text is co-authored by David Lien, a graduate of Westmont College and Dallas Theological Seminary. He also wrote the Living Insights sections.

Editor in Chief:
Cynthia Swindoll

Coauthor of Text:
David Lien

Assistant Editor:
Wendy Peterson

Copy Editors:
Connie Laser,
Glenda Schlahta

Designer:
Gary Lett

Production Artists:
Renee Dallas, Gary Lett

Typographer:
Bob Haskins

Director, Communications Division:
Deedee Snyder

Project Manager:
Alene Cooper

Project Supervisor:
Susan Nelson

Project Assistant:
Ellen Galey

Print Production Manager:
John Norton

Printer:
Sinclair Printing Company

Unless otherwise identified, all Scripture references are from the New American Standard Bible, © The Lockman Foundation 1960, 1962, 1963, 1968, 1971, 1972, 1973, 1975, 1977. Used by permission. The other translation cited is the New International Version (NIV).

An effort has been made to locate sources and obtain permission where necessary for the quotations used in this book. In the event of any unintentional omission, a modification will gladly be incorporated in future printings.

ISBN 0-8499-8433-5
Printed in the United States of America.
COVER: Victoria and Albert/Art Resource, N.Y.

CONTENTS

INTRODUCTION

No one was more respected, more feared, or more significant to the ancient Jews than those who stood before the people as God's prophets. When the prophet spoke, the people listened. Their words had impact, like bullets spinning out of a rifle, drilling their way into the heart. Prophets had clout! They weren't always appreciated, but they were seldom ignored.

And no one can deny that Elijah was one of the greatest. He was God's lightning during the dark days under Ahab and Jezebel's rule. Suddenly he appeared . . . and almost as mysteriously he disappeared into the sky. But sandwiched between his entrance and his exit, Elijah left an indelible mark etched upon his times.

In no way, however, should we think of him as superhuman. One of the New Testament writers states, "Elijah was a man with a nature like ours . . ." (James 5:17). Again and again we'll identify with his humanity, which (hopefully) will encourage us throughout these biographical snapshots.

Let's listen and learn. Elijah's life and times are as relevant to this generation as those whose names appear in today's newspaper. Perhaps more so!

Chuck Swindoll

Chuck Swindoll

PUTTING TRUTH INTO ACTION

Knowledge apart from application falls short of God's desire for His children. He wants us to apply what we learn so that we will change and grow. This study guide was prepared with these goals in mind. As you go through the following pages, we hope your desire to discover biblical truth will grow as your understanding of God's Word increases, and that you will be encouraged to apply what you've learned.

To assist you in your study, we've included a section called **Living Insights** at the end of each lesson. These exercises will challenge you to study further and to think of specific ways to put your discoveries into action.

There are many ways to use this guide—in personal devotions, group studies, discussions with friends and family, and Sunday school classes. And, of course, it's an ideal study aid when you're listening to its corresponding "Insight for Living" radio series.

To benefit most from this study guide, we would encourage you to consider it a spiritual journal. That's why we've included space in the **Living Insights** for recording your thoughts and discoveries. We hope you'll return to those sections often for review and encouragement as you continue to grow in your walk with Christ.

David Lien
Coauthor of Text
Author of Living Insights

The
Life and
Times of
Elijah

Chapter 1

STANDING ALONE
IN THE GAP

1 Kings 16:29–17:1

O f all the prophets who blazed across ancient Israel's history, none burned as radiantly as Elijah.

J. Oswald Sanders likened him to a meteor that "flashed across the inky blackness of Israel's spiritual night."[1] And Matthew Henry wrote that

> never was Israel so blessed with a good prophet as
> when it was so plagued with a bad king. Never was
> king so bold to sin as Ahab; never was prophet so
> bold to reprove and threaten as Elijah. . . . He only,
> of all the prophets, had the honor of Enoch, the
> first prophet, to be translated, that he should not see
> death, and the honor of Moses, the great prophet,
> to attend our Savior in his transfiguration. Other
> prophets prophesied and wrote, he prophesied and
> acted, but wrote nothing; but his actions cast more
> luster on his name than their writings did on theirs.[2]

Who was Elijah? And what set him apart? To gain an understanding of this fiery prophet, whose comet trail we'll be tracing through the next ten studies, we must first understand the times in which he lived.

---

1. J. Oswald Sanders, *Robust in Faith* (Chicago, Ill.: Moody Press, 1965), p. 125.

2. Matthew Henry, *Commentary on the Whole Bible*, one-volume ed. (Grand Rapids, Mich.: Zondervan Publishing House, Regency Reference Library, 1961), p. 385.

The Times of Elijah

The steel of a person's character is forged on the anvil of one's times. And often, the darker the times are, the brighter the soul that stands against them shines.

We need only think of such people as Abraham Lincoln, steering our country through the darkness of the Civil War; Winston Churchill, rallying England—and the world—to never give in until the deep night of Nazism was broken through; and Corrie ten Boom, showing generations how to scatter the blackness of hate with the lamp of God's forgiveness and love.

These were bright lights in decadent times, brilliant stars cast against a darkened sky. And few skies were darker in Israel's history than the one against which Elijah flung his faith.

Generally—the Kings of Israel

Saul, David, and Solomon, each in their turn, had ruled a unified Hebrew nation for more than one hundred years. But when Solomon's son Rehoboam ascended the throne, he foolishly oppressed the people with heavy taxes and conscription labor, which prompted civil war (1 Kings 12:1–24). The result? A north-south division. The northern people were known as Israel, while the southerners were called Judah. This Israel-Judah distinction carries through Scripture until Israel (the north) is defeated by the Assyrians and Judah, (the south) is sacked by Babylon. This period between the split and the Babylonian captivity is known as the time of the kings. Some of those kings were good; most were evil.

A brief survey of the northern kings leading up to Elijah's time will show us what this man of God was up against.

Jeroboam. While Rehoboam continued to rule Judah, Jeroboam became the first king of the new northern nation of Israel. An evil man, he led the people away from God and into idolatry.

> He made priests of the high places from among all
> the people. . . . And this event became sin to the
> house of Jeroboam, even to blot it out and destroy
> it from off the face of the earth. (13:33b–34)

A poor beginning for northern leadership. This infamous ruler produced a ground swell of murder, deception, and religious perversion that ran throughout the entire line of Israel's kings.

Nadab. This son of Jeroboam fanned the same idolatrous coals his father started.

> And he did evil in the sight of the Lord, and walked
> in the way of his father and in his sin which he made
> Israel sin. (15:26)

His two-year reign ended in his murder (v. 27).

Baasha. A paranoid mass murderer, he killed Nadab, then wiped out anyone associated with Jeroboam's previous dynasty, establishing a twenty-four-year reign of evil (vv. 28–29, 33).

> And he did evil in the sight of the Lord, and walked
> in the way of Jeroboam and in his sin which he made
> Israel sin. (v. 34)

Elah. While in a drunken stupor, this son of Baasha was assassinated by his servant Zimri after only two short years of rule.

> Thus Zimri destroyed all the household of Baasha
> . . . for all the sins of Baasha and the sins of Elah
> his son, which they sinned and which they made
> Israel sin, provoking the Lord God of Israel to anger
> with their idols. (16:12–13)

Zimri. Having murdered the king and all his house *and* Baasha's house, Zimri was next to sit on Israel's throne. What followed is incredible. Zimri ruled for only *one week* before the people begged Omri, the commander of the army, to be their king (vv. 15–16). He complied and laid siege to Zimri's city; and Zimri, in desperation, committed suicide (vv. 17–18). Scripture's same mournful refrain sums up his life like the rest.

> He sinned, doing evil in the sight of the Lord, walk-
> ing in the way of Jeroboam, and in his sin which he
> did, making Israel sin. (v. 19)

Omri. After several years, Omri managed to bring some semblance of stability to Israel. He never sought the Lord, though; in fact, he exceeded all his predecessors in evil acts (vv. 21–25).

> For he walked in all the way of Jeroboam . . . and
> in his sins which he made Israel sin, provoking the
> Lord God of Israel with their idols. (v. 26)

For more than half a century, intrigue, bloodshed, conspiracy, and immorality permeated Israel's entire social infrastructure. And for all of those years, the insidious tendrils of idolatry had slowly spread over the nation and put their roots down deep.

3

The darkness was terrible, but it was about to get worse as Omri's son Ahab ascended the throne.

Specifically—Ahab and Jezebel

Ahab has a unique distinction in the annals of the kings.

> Ahab the son of Omri did evil in the sight of the Lord *more* than all who were before him. . . . Ahab did *more* to provoke the Lord God of Israel than all the kings of Israel who were before him. (vv. 30, 33b, emphasis added)

The account of Ahab's reign is also the first among the kings to elaborate on a marriage (v. 31). And for good reason.

> By himself Ahab would have been a menace. . . . Plainly an opportunist, he seems to have had few convictions or scruples. But he was not by himself. Jezebel was by his side, using her prestige and influence as insidiously and maliciously as possible. Like Solomon's foreign wives, she continued her pagan worship, maintaining it on a lavish scale. When the prophets of Yahweh opposed her heathen ways, she set out viciously to destroy them, ruthlessly and thoroughly. . . .
>
> Having bent every effort to suppress true prophetic activity, Jezebel imported to her court hundreds of false prophets dedicated to Baal. . . . Such zeal in so strategic a position posed an incalculable threat to Israel's historic faith. The corruption of Canaanite religion had long been seeping in from the Israelites' Canaanite neighbors, but under Jezebel it was pumped from the palace with extraordinary pressure.[3]

Jezebel, her name long synonymous with wickedness, will be Elijah's chief foe. For it is she who rules her husband and, therefore, the nation. And it is her god Baal who challenges the one true God for the souls of His people.[4]

---

3. William Sanford LaSor, David Allan Hubbard, and Frederic William Bush, *Old Testament Survey* (Grand Rapids, Mich.: William B. Eerdmans Publishing Co., 1982), p. 266.

4. Baal was a god of many faces, being a god of rain, fertility, and the personification of the sun. "The worship of Baal . . . one of the oldest superstitions in the world, was the

Person of Elijah

Into this scene of darkness and degradation steps Elijah, who is not afraid to shine the light of God's Word right into Ahab's eyes.

> Now Elijah the Tishbite, who was of the settlers of Gilead, said to Ahab, "As the Lord, the God of Israel lives, before whom I stand, surely there shall be neither dew nor rain these years, except by my word." (17:1)

Such a confrontation is headlines, prime-time TV news! No one confronts the royal couple and lives to tell about it. What kind of person is this who challenges Israel's court?

Just a man—a very simple man who loved God more than his own life.

His Name

Elijah's name is the first clue to his identity, because it encapsulates his life's focus, authority, and message. Meaning "my God is Jehovah," his name

> states succinctly the theme of his ministry. In an age characterized by easy tolerance and open assimilation to Canaanite religion, Elijah asserts his personal determination ("My God" is emphatic) to keep the First Commandment. It is to bring the northern kingdom to a like determination that his ministry is directed.[5]

His Land

Elijah's homeland also offers us insight into his identity. He was a "Tishbite, who was of the settlers of Gilead" (v. 1). This area east of the Jordan River is known for its harshness—rocky valleys and austere mountains form a jagged landscape that provides little shelter

---

worship of the sun, regarded as the king of heaven. The Baalim were the gods of the land, owning and controlling it, and the increase of crops, fruit and cattle was supposed to be under their control." Worshiping him included offering incense and sacrifices—sometimes of children—and performing perverse and degrading sexual acts. See Sanders, *Robust in Faith*, p. 126.

5. Gene Rice, *Nations Under God: A Commentary on the Book of 1 Kings*, International Theological Commentary series (Grand Rapids, Mich.: William B. Eerdmans Publishing Co., 1990), p. 141.

from the hot desert sun. It is a solitary place; its ruggedness is reflected in Elijah's leathery character—hard, unpolished, humble. And yet Elijah was a man of compelling tenderness, which we shall see as his life unfolds in the studies to come.

His Style

Elijah's speech to Ahab in verse 1b reveals his style.

> "As the Lord, the God of Israel lives, before whom I stand, surely there shall be neither dew nor rain these years, except by my word."

Simple, direct, free of malice, his words show him to be a man zealous for God yet tender before Him. He seems to have lived standing in God's presence, which made the Lord more real to him than all the opposition of his day.

So few of us stand as Elijah did. We have learned, consciously or unconsciously, the way of the chameleon—we blend ourselves into the scenery of our times. Often, our tolerance and long-suffering border on compromise, making us ineffective as Christ's lights in a dark world. But we needn't stay in that obscurity. We can learn, like Elijah, to flash "across the inky blackness" of our times and light up the sky with God's message of righteousness and love.

Lessons from Elijah

Elijah's life is rich with lessons for us; in fact, from just this introduction to him we can glean at least three.

God looks for special people at difficult times. God found Elijah, not among the royal family nor anyone near Ahab or Jezebel, but in rugged, remote Gilead. Position, power, connections—none of these are God's criteria for choosing a servant. Rather, He looks for individuals who are ready instruments—those who stand out brightly against the backdrop of corrupt times (see Ezek. 22:30; see also 2 Chron. 16:9 and Phil. 2:15).

God's methods are often surprising. One person, not an army, was sufficient to confront the whole Israelite government. God could have orchestrated another inside assassination, but that would not have revealed His heart for His people. Instead, He chose Elijah. Elijah, all alone, was the best strategy to use against the royal couple because of his uncompromising loyalty to God. Have you ever thought that perhaps *you* are God's chosen method in His unconventional warfare?

God wants us to stand before Him, first and foremost. Elijah's first words to Ahab reveal the prophet's focus: "As the Lord, the God of Israel lives, before whom I stand . . ." (1 Kings 17:1). Because he was ever conscious of God's presence, Elijah was able to face Ahab without fear. We, too, can face our Ahabs without fear, if we will irradiate our souls with an Elijah-like perspective of our Lord. Let the words of another prophet, Isaiah, begin to accustom your eyes to the brilliance of God.

> Thus says God the Lord,
> Who created the heavens and stretched them out,
> Who spread out the earth and its offspring,
> Who gives breath to the people on it,
> And spirit to those who walk in it,
> "I am the Lord, I have called you in righteousness,
> I will also hold you by the hand and watch over you,
> And I will appoint you as a covenant to the people,
> As a light to the nations,
> To open blind eyes,
> To bring out prisoners from the dungeon,
> And those who dwell in darkness from the prison."
> (Isa. 42:5–7)

As we trace the star streaks of Elijah's life in the days ahead, let the Creator of light, the Light of the World, burn brightly in your heart so that you can illumine your dark and stumbling world, as Elijah did his.

Living Insights   STUDY ONE

Remember the night when, as a child, you had to take the trash outside when it was pitch black? Your mind thinks funny things in darkness. It begins when you step out of the house's warm light and venture into territory that, just hours earlier, was daylight safe. But now this same area is completely transformed into a world of monsters lurking behind corners, trees, and bushes.

As Christians, we sometimes feel this way when we leave our softly lit sanctuaries and venture out into the world. The terrors of *that* night, however, are quite real, just as they were in the prophet Ezekiel's time.

And the word of the Lord came to me saying, "Son of man, say to her, 'You are a land that is not cleansed or rained on in the day of indignation.' There is conspiracy of her prophets in her midst, like a roaring lion tearing the prey. They have devoured lives; they have taken treasure and precious things; they have made many widows in the midst of her. Her priests have done violence to My law and have profaned My holy things; they have made no distinction between the holy and the profane, and they have not taught the difference between the unclean and the clean; and they hide their eyes from My sabbaths, and I am profaned among them. Her princes within her are like wolves tearing the prey, by shedding blood and destroying lives in order to get dishonest gain. And her prophets have smeared whitewash for them, seeing false visions and divining lies for them, saying, 'Thus says the Lord God,' when the Lord has not spoken. The people of the land have practiced oppression and committed robbery, and they have wronged the poor and needy and have oppressed the sojourner without justice." (Ezek. 22:23–29)

Not too different from our day, is it? In fact, why don't you take a few moments to write down some of the dark characteristics that our times share with Ezekiel's.

_____   _____

_____   _____

_____   _____

Does your mind do funny things in the midst of this darkness? What thoughts and feelings surface when you encounter the situations you listed above?

_____

_____

_____

_____

Sometimes we can be paralyzed by fear, or worse, hardened by a hopeless indifference. Perhaps that was the case in Ezekiel's era, for the Lord

> "searched for a man among them who should build up the wall and stand in the gap before Me for the land, that I should not destroy it; but I found no one." (v. 30)

In Ahab and Jezebel's day, God did find someone to stand in the gap: Elijah. How about in your day?

Our sanctuaries are safe places—and rightly so. But the whole of a Christian's life is not lived in the sanctuary; it is also lived in the world. Are you willing, like Elijah, to stand in the gap and pierce the darkness with the light of God's message? In what spheres can you begin to do this?

_____

_____

_____

As you explore this question, take along some encouragement from the apostle John: "You are from God, little children, and have overcome them; because greater is He who is in you than he who is in the world" (1 John 4:4).

🍇 *Living Insights* STUDY TWO

"Have you ever wondered why there is so much in the Scriptures that is biographical? It is obvious to even a casual reader of this Book that its pages are penetrated with personality—men and women who are not fugitives from a wax museum but who are made of the same tissue of life as each of us. The Holy Spirit loves to teach truth in terms of life."[6]

As we enter the Spirit's school of truth through this series, let's get an overview of our course by reading ahead about the life and times of Elijah. The pertinent texts will be 1 Kings 17–19, 21; and

---

6. Howard G. Hendricks, *Elijah: Confrontation, Conflict, and Crisis* (Chicago, Ill.: Moody Press, 1972), p. 5.

2 Kings 1–2. For extra credit, explore Matthew 17:1–8; Luke 9:28–36; and James 5:17–18. Use the space provided to write down insights you discover and questions that come up. Whatever you do, get to know this meteoric man through whom God will be speaking to you in the days ahead!

_____

_____

_____

_____

_____

_____

_____

_____

_____

_____

_____

Chapter 2

BOOT CAMP AT CHERITH

1 Kings 17:1–7

*B*oot camp. The very words conjure up images of freshly stubbled heads, dog tags, fatigues—and fatigue. For here a civilian is molded into a soldier through the rigors of push-ups, sit-ups, running, marching, and double time, courtesy of the drill sergeant. Control of one's life is left at the induction center, and the raw recruit is shaped into military fitness at another's hands.

As tough as this is, there really isn't any other way to achieve the desired—and necessary—results. You just don't learn how to survive on a battlefield by bubbling around in a Jacuzzi and ringing for room service.

What's true in military life is also true in spiritual life, to a certain extent. When we first believe, we become soldiers in God's "army." But we aren't really fit for battle until we've had some basic training.

Even the great prophet Elijah went through boot camp, which effectively turned that simple Tishbite into a man of God (1 Kings 17:1, 24). In today's lesson, let's follow him through his time of training and pick up a few pointers along the way for our own boot camps.

The Pronouncement of Drought

Let's begin our study at the place where Elijah is still known as "the Tishbite" and take a look at the event that precipitates the prophet's boot camp experience.

> Now Elijah the Tishbite, who was of the settlers of Gilead, said to Ahab, "As the Lord, the God of Israel lives, before whom I stand, surely there shall be neither dew nor rain these years, except by my word." (v. 1)

There are two things to notice in this verse: first, that Elijah is making a prophecy; and second, whom the prophecy is really from. Elijah warns the ruling couple that their domain will be refreshed by not a drop of rain or even dew for "these years." Not a few weeks, not a few months—but *years*. Farms would fail, famine would stalk

11

the land, and Baal's cult of deceit would face the challenge of all time. And how did Elijah muster the courage to deliver this dreadful message to the murderous, Jehovah-hating king and queen? He was empowered by the Living Lord, the initiator of the prophecy.

Elijah must have been itching to run through the city of Samaria declaring God's judgment, hoping to shake the people up and get their attention. But God had other plans.

God Told Him What to Do

> And the word of the Lord came to him, saying, "Go away from here and turn eastward, and hide yourself by the brook Cherith, which is east[1] of the Jordan." (vv. 2–3)

Two reasons for this command come to mind: first, it was for Elijah's *protection*. If you skip ahead to verse 10 of chapter 18, you'll find that "there was no nation or kingdom" where the wrathful Ahab had "not sent to search" for the prophet. And second, it was for Elijah's *training*, to provide his time alone with God in boot camp.

For some of us, one of the most difficult commands we can ever hear and obey is the command to be alone, to get away from the spotlight. As unsettling as it seems, though, moving away from public life to the privacy of the brook is sometimes God's best for us. An essential part of becoming a man or woman of God is to learn contentment in the humble places of life, as commentator A. W. Pink explains.

> The prophet needed further training in secret if he was to be personally fitted to speak again for God in public. Ah, my reader, the man whom the Lord uses has to be kept low. . . . How humbling! Alas, how little is man to be trusted: how little is he able to bear being put into the place of honor! How quickly self rises to the surface, and the instrument is ready to believe he is something more than an

---

1. The exact location of the brook Cherith is unknown. Some commentators believe it was literally east of the Jordan River, putting Elijah in territory that would have been familiar to him; while others think that the word *east* is better translated "in the face of," "before," or "towards," which would put him on the western side of the Jordan. Therefore maps and commentaries will vary according to their resolve on the use of this word *east*. See C.F. Keil and F. Delitzsch, *Commentary on the Old Testament*, trans. James Martin (reprint, Grand Rapids, Mich.: William B. Eerdmans Publishing Co., 1978), vol. 3, p. 236.

instrument. How sadly easy it is to make of the very service God entrusts us with a pedestal on which to display ourselves.[2]

God Told Him How He'd Survive

"And it shall be that you shall drink of the brook, and I have commanded the ravens to provide for you there." (17:4)

Rather than having to serve KP duty, Elijah gets God's own unique catering service in this boot camp! There's an important lesson to learn here, aside from the reminder of God's miraculous creativity. And this is the reminder that God will provide—He knows our needs and tenderly meets them, even during our times by the brook.

The Obedience of Elijah

With no hint of hesitation, Elijah does his part.

So he went and did according to the word of the Lord, for he went and lived by the brook Cherith, which is east of the Jordan. (v. 5)

Several days alone in the wilderness is called a retreat. But when days roll over into months, *hermitage* may be a more descriptive term. Yet Elijah, in all his loneliness, could not improve upon the brook Cherith for the effect it would have on his life.

God, too, does His part for this obedient servant.

And the ravens brought him bread and meat in the morning and bread and meat in the evening, and he would drink from the brook. (v. 6)

Cool, clear water; each day his daily bread; and unbroken communion with God. Though perhaps stark, this is a peaceful scene. Until . . .

the brook dried up, because there was no rain in the land. (v. 7)

The brook dried up. But God had told Elijah to come here—it was part of His plan! And the prophet had obeyed so swiftly, so

2. Arthur W. Pink, *The Life of Elijah* (Swengel, Pa.: Bible Truth Depot, 1956), p. 41.

trustingly. What was God doing? F. B. Meyer assures us that God knew exactly what He was doing, for "God's servants are often called to sit by drying brooks."

> Many of us have had to sit by drying brooks; perhaps some are sitting by them now—the drying brook of popularity, ebbing away as it did from John the Baptist. The drying brook of health, sinking under a creeping paralysis, or a slow decline. The drying brook of money, slowly dwindling before the demands of sickness, bad debts, or other people's extravagance. The drying brook of friendship, which for long has been diminishing, and threatens soon to cease. Ah, it is hard to sit beside a drying brook. . . .
>
> Why does God let them dry? He wants to teach us not to trust in his gifts but in himself. Let us learn these lessons, and turn from our failing Cheriths to our unfailing Savior. All sufficiency resides in him.[3]

The Lessons of Cherith

If the water of your brook is at trickle level—or even dry—take heart that, far from forgetting you, God is actually keenly interested in your development. He uses times like these to teach us eternal lessons, just as He did for Elijah.

Lessons for Elijah

Elijah, though a courageous and God-fearing prophet, still had a couple of things to learn.

First: *He needed to learn that the same God who gives water can choose to take water away.* That is God's sovereign right. We, however, have the feeling that once He gives water, He should never take it back. That once He gives a mate or a child, a business or a ministry, He should never take it back. When He does, we feel forgotten and not cared for. But Isaiah reassures us that God never forgets those who love Him.

> But Zion said, "The Lord has forsaken me,
> And the Lord has forgotten me."

3. F. B. Meyer, *Great Men of the Bible* (London, England: Marshall Pickering, 1990), pp. 345–46.

"Can a woman forget her nursing child,
And have no compassion on the son of her womb?
Even these may forget, but I will not forget you.
Behold, I have inscribed you on the palms of My
hands." (Isa. 49:14–16a)

God's sovereignty and His care go hand in hand with boot camp.

Elijah's second lesson was this: *The dried-up brook was a direct result of his own prayer.* Day by day, while he watched the brook dwindle into a trickle, then trickle into a puddle, then puddle into nothing more than dry ground, Elijah was witnessing prophecy realized and prayer answered. As James tells us:

> Elijah was a man with a nature like ours, and he prayed earnestly that it might not rain; and it did not rain. (James 5:17a)

He had asked God for a drought, and he got one. What a time for rejoicing! Yet . . . what a time for getting caught short.

Yes, Elijah was experiencing the result of his prayer; but it hurt. Have you ever prayed to become more like Christ, but then asked God not to let it hurt too much? To become patient, but only if it didn't take too long? To learn humility, but only if it didn't make you too uncomfortable? Remember, God's spiritual boot camp is not designed for our comfort—it is designed for our spiritual growth and maturity. And sometimes that involves pain.

Lessons for Us

From Elijah's story we can take to heart at least four things.

First: *We must be as willing to be set aside as to be used.* F. B. Meyer calls this "the value of the hidden life," a life that teaches us our place in God's plan and compels us "in the sequestered vale of some Cherith" to examine our motives. He adds that every Christian who

> would wield great power with people must win it in some hidden Cherith. We cannot give out unless we have previously taken in. . . . Not one of us can dispense with a Cherith where we may taste the sweets and imbibe the power of a life hidden with Christ, and in Christ by the power of the Holy Ghost.[4]

4. Meyer, *Great Men of the Bible*, p. 344.

So when God wants you to learn at His feet, don't chafe at being hidden. Instead, follow His command to "be still, and know that [He is] God" (Ps. 46:10 NIV).

Second: *God's direction includes provision.* God told Elijah to go to the brook; and when he got there he found safety, quietness, cool water to drink . . . and a menu planned by ravens. Not exactly the chefs we would have chosen, but who better to carry food to a re-mote hiding place and not blab to anyone about it? God's ways of providing are often surprising to us, but they are always the best ways.

Third: *We are to trust our God one day at a time.* Did you notice in this passage that God never told Elijah the next step until he had taken the first one? Elijah faced each day and each challenge one at a time. Commentator John R. W. Stott would call this approach to life an antidote to worry.

> Worry is a waste—a waste of time, thought and nervous energy. We need to learn to live a day at a time. . . . "Each day has troubles enough of its own" [Matt. 6:34]. So why anticipate them? If we do, we double them. For if our [object of] fear does not ma-terialize, we have worried once for nothing; if it does materialize, we have worried twice instead of once. In both cases it is foolish: worry doubles trouble.[5]

And fourth: *A dried-up brook is often a sign of God's pleasure, not His disappointment, in our walk with Him.* Had Elijah done anything wrong that he needed to be disciplined for? No; he had been praying fervently that God would intervene in Israel's idolatry (James 5:17), and he had fearlessly faced Ahab in obedience to the Lord's word. God led Elijah by the brook—the dried-up brook—to further shape and refine His willing servant's faith.[6]

Our faith is precious to God, "more precious than gold which is perishable, even though tested by fire" (1 Pet. 1:7a); and even if it takes a boot camp experience or a long, dusty spell beside a dry brook, God will refine our faith until we're "found to result in praise and glory and honor at the revelation of Jesus Christ" (v. 7b). Doesn't that make it all worthwhile?

5. John R. W. Stott, *The Message of the Sermon on the Mount (Matthew 5–7): Christian Counter-Culture,* rev. ed. (Downers Grove, Ill.: Inter-Varsity Press, 1978), p. 169.

6. Several other men who pleased God also found themselves beside a dry brook: Abraham, at the sacrifice of Isaac (Gen. 22); Joseph, in an Egyptian prison on a false charge (Gen. 39); and Paul, in Lystra after being stoned and left for dead (Acts 14).

Set aside, hidden, humbled, led to a drying brook. Many of us can identify with Elijah's sojourn at Cherith. But have we understood what God was doing for us in our own Cheriths? Have we gained any insight into the way God prepares us for a deeper relationship with Him and further service for Him? Perhaps if we were to see it in black and white, it would make more sense.

Here's an idea of what God's training method looks like. Keep in mind that each *line* represents a barrier of resistance to God's instruction, and each *space* shows a stage of development through which God wants to take us once the barrier is broken.

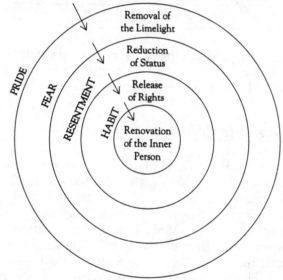

Before God can accustom us to the Light of the World, He must first remove the artifical limelight that pride shines in our eyes.

Before God can bring us to the nourishing pastures of humility, He must first take down the cardboard backdrop of status that our fears prop up.

Before God can hand us the things He would give us freely, He must first pry loose our fingers on the rights our resentments hold fast.

And before God can enlarge our hearts, He must first renew our inner person by knocking loose the habits that constrict and block the flow of life.

Where are you in God's training program? Is there a certain barrier you are struggling with? What has this been like for you?

_____

_____

_____

Which stage of development are you in the midst of? What are some of the lessons God has taught you here?

_____

_____

_____

Though often challenging and sometimes painful, God's training method always has a purpose. Remember, it brought Elijah from being just a "Tishbite" to being "a man of God."

🍇 *Living Insights*   STUDY TWO

Boot camp is hard enough; but when your brook dries up too, it can feel unendurable. Notice, though, that it only *feels* this way. What you may feel is coming to destroy you may actually be here to make you. Richard Seume, in his book *Shoes for the Road*, relates a story written by the late Vance Havner that illustrates this truth.

A community of farmers who were raising cotton in the Deep South faced ruin as their crops were devastated by the merciless boll weevil. The poorhouse loomed in everyone's future, unless the farmers could come up with a plan to turn the situation around. Being the ingenious lot that farmers are, that's just what they did. They planted peanuts and other crops that boll weevils don't have a taste for, and they made more money than they'd ever made raising cotton. So what had at first seemed like disaster turned into a boon. And out of gratitude for the incident that brought about their good fortune, they built a monument to the boll weevil!

Out of this story Havner then made the following application.

> "All things work together for good" to the Christian, even our boll weevil experiences. Sometimes we settle into a humdrum routine as monotonous as

growing cotton year after year. Then God sends the boll weevil; He jolts us out of our groove, and we must find new ways to live. Financial reverses, great bereavement, physical infirmity, loss of position—how many have been driven by trouble to be better husbandmen and to bring forth far finer fruit from their souls! The best thing that ever happened to some of us was the coming of our "boll weevil." Without that we might still have been a "cotton sharecropper."

If the boll weevil has struck your cotton crop, do not despair. The day may come when you will put up a monument to the bane that became a blessing.[7]

Has the boll weevil struck your cotton crop? Has your once bubbling brook inexplicably dried up? Don't despair. Take it, as Elijah did, one day at a time, and remember that God *will* work it out for your ultimate good. You have His Word on that.

7. Vance Havner, *It Is Toward Evening,* as quoted by Richard H. Seume in *Shoes for the Road* (Chicago, Ill.: Moody Press, 1974), p. 87.

Chapter 3
ADVANCED TRAINING AT ZAREPHATH
1 Kings 17:8–16

Hot, still, dry . . . brook Cherith, in its quiet loneliness, was both a refuge and a refinery for Elijah. Here he was hidden from Ahab; and here he was honed by isolation. Here he rested in the presence of God; and here he struggled with his humbling dependence. Here his needs were met by God's provision; and here his brook dried up.

Was this the end of the road for Elijah? Would God leave His faithful servant beside a cracked and sandy riverbed, letting his body and spirit become parched? No, not the God of answered prayers, fulfilled prophecy, and met needs. This was not the end of Elijah's road, just the beginning of another. For when that brook dried up:

> Then the word of the Lord came to him, saying, "Arise, go to Zarephath, which belongs to Sidon, and stay there; behold, I have commanded a widow there to provide for you." (1 Kings 17:8–9)

So to Zarephath Elijah went (v. 10a). And it is to Zarephath, where Elijah will enter into more advanced training than at Cherith, [1] that we will go to learn the lessons God will teach him there.

Experience at Zarephath

What kind of an experience will Zarephath be? Perhaps the name of the place itself provides a clue. The root word in verb form means "smelt, refine, test"; in the noun form, it means "crucible." [2] Advanced training indeed.

---

1. Interestingly, the root form of the noun Cherith means to "cut off, cut down" either things or people. William Gesenius, A Hebrew and English Lexicon of the Old Testament, trans. Edward Robinson, ed. Francis Brown, S. R. Driver, Charles A. Briggs (1907; reprint, Oxford, England: At the Clarendon Press, 1962), p. 503. It conveys the idea of scraping, filing, whittling, or removing, which describes the process Elijah went through by the brook.

2. Gesenius, Robinson, et al., Hebrew and English Lexicon, p. 864.

God's Command

Let's take a closer look at God's directives in verses 8–9. Verse 8 tells us:

> Then the word of the Lord came to him.

At first glance, this seems like a simple transition to keep the story moving along. But three little words, "came to him," speak volumes about God's care for Elijah. They tell us that *God knew where he was*. As the brook trickled away into sand, it's possible that Elijah thought God had lost track of him. But, of course, He had not, and God reassured him of this by coming to Elijah rather than letting the prophet anxiously search for Him.

Once the Lord came, He told Elijah,

> "Arise, go to Zarephath, which belongs to Sidon,
> and stay there; behold, I have commanded a widow
> there to provide for you." (v. 9)

From this verse we learn another important truth: *God knew where he was going*. Elijah didn't know what would happen after Cherith, just as we don't know our futures either. But God does, and He makes sure that we're provided for.

So far, Zarephath doesn't sound like much of a crucible. But consider whom God appointed to provide for Elijah: a widow. It probably would have been much easier for Elijah if God had commanded him to provide for the widow instead of the other way around. Widows were vulnerable in that society, as Herbert Lockyer tells us:

> The lot of widows who, from earliest times wore
> a distinctive garb . . . was generally precarious. . . .
> Deprived of husband and protector, a widow was
> exposed to all sorts of mean actions and extortions,
> hence laws to protect her and to uphold her cause.[3]

And now Elijah—an independent loner from rough-and-tumble Gilead who had stood before the king—must further humble himself by allowing this bereaved and needy person to take care of him. The smelting has begun.

---

3. Herbert Lockyer, *All the Women of the Bible* (Grand Rapids, Mich.: Zondervan Publishing House, n.d.), p. 17.

Elijah's Obedience

Having been given the go-ahead from God, Elijah sets out for Zarephath (v. 10a). It's a long walk, taking him across wilderness, through Ahab's terrain, to a Gentile city on the Mediterranean coast of southern Sidon—Jezebel's home country (16:31). And all along the way, the pallor of drought settling deep into Israel's soil is his constant companion.

Finally he reaches the gates of the little city, and

> behold, a widow was there gathering sticks; and he called to her and said, "Please get me a little water in a jar, that I may drink." And as she was going to get it, he called to her and said, "Please bring me a piece of bread in your hand." But she said, "As the Lord your God lives, I have no bread, only a handful of flour in the bowl and a little oil in the jar; and behold, I am gathering a few sticks that I may go in and prepare for me and my son, that we may eat it and die." (17:10b–12)

Who would be providing for Elijah? Not just any widow, but a starving widow with a hungry boy to take care of . . . an impoverished widow preparing the last meal for herself and her son . . . a bereaved widow whose hope had died. Elijah has now encountered the first of two tests: *the test of first impressions.*

What would he do—turn back to Cherith? Did the dry brook look more promising than this? Maybe he could find himself another hiding place. Perhaps God meant another widow; surely He couldn't have meant this one—this woman who was hardly capable of taking care of herself and her son! And he's just asked to eat their last meal too.

Remembering his Cherith cuisine a la ravens, however, Elijah stays where God told him to stay and proceeds to enter his next test: *the test of physical impossibility.*

The woman's eyes, understandably, were on the handful of flour in the bowl and the little bit of oil in the jar. It was physically impossible to keep two people, let alone three, alive on that scant amount of food. But Elijah's eyes were on the God who provides.

> Then Elijah said to her, "Do not fear; go, do as you have said, but make me a little bread cake from it first, and bring it out to me, and afterward you may

make one for yourself and for your son. For thus says the Lord God of Israel, 'The bowl of flour shall not be exhausted, nor shall the jar of oil be empty, until the day that the Lord sends rain on the face of the earth.'" (vv. 13–14)

How can Elijah say this? Because he *knows* from personal experience, not secondhand stories or academic theories, that God comes through when He says He will. And it is his faith, his certainty, that enables the widow to put her trust in his God also.

So she went and did according to the word of Elijah. (v. 15a)

God's Faithfulness

And she was not disappointed.

And she and he and her household ate for many days. The bowl of flour was not exhausted nor did the jar of oil become empty, according to the word of the Lord which He spoke through Elijah. (vv. 15b–16)

Granted, their menu would not make the favorite recipes section of *Bon Appétit* magazine—biscuits and water in the morning and water and biscuits in the evening—but their *needs* were miraculously met!

This display of God's faithfulness could not help but affect this formerly starving and desperate widow. Can't you just imagine Elijah getting up one morning and hearing her fix breakfast?

Crackle, crackle, hiss.

"Praise God from whom all blessings flow . . ."

Clatter, clatter, whoosh.

". . . Praise Him, all creatures here below . . ."

Stir, stir, stir.

". . . Praise Him above, ye heav'nly host . . ."

Sizzle, sizzle, flip.

". . . Praise Father, Son and Holy Ghost!"[4]

That widow met God in her kitchen! She looked into that bowl, and she found flour. She looked into that jar, and she found oil. Morning and evening, day in and day out, she witnessed God providing. You can be sure that more than her body was nourished.

---

4. Thomas Ken, "Doxology," from *The Hymnal for Worship and Celebration* (Waco, Tex.: Word Music, 1986), no. 625.

Lessons for Today

As we prepare to leave Elijah and the widow at Zarephath, let's linger over four lessons we can take with us when we enter a time of advanced training.

First: *God's leading is often surprising—don't analyze it.* If God tells you to go to Zarephath, then go—whether you can make sense out of it or not. If He leads you to stay in that situation, even though it may be very difficult, then stay there—don't rack your brain trying to figure out God's thinking. We are finite, remember, and God is infinite. He can see the whole picture, where we are only aware of fragmentary glimpses.

Second: *The beginning days are often the hardest—don't quit.* Remember Elijah's test of the first impression? If he'd given up then, everyone might have starved and God would have been robbed of an opportunity to lovingly provide for His people. Usually, the first days of a new situation are the hardest; it won't be that tough the whole time. So don't quit.

Third: *God's promises often hinge on obedience—don't ignore your part.* Elijah was commanded to "arise, go, . . . and stay there" (v. 9). The widow was told to "go . . . make me a little bread cake from [the flour and oil] first" (v. 13). In each case, obedience preceded God's provision, so remember to do your part too when God promises to provide for you.

Fourth: *God's provisions are often just enough—don't fail to thank Him.* Biscuits and water aren't exactly a smorgasbord of delights, but they filled hungry stomachs and sustained that household throughout a devastating drought. Have you thanked God for the ways He has met your needs? A grateful heart not only gives appreciation where it is due but also enriches the one who possesses it.

A Concluding Thought

So far we've seen Elijah in Cherith's boot camp of obscurity and Zarephath's crucible of humility. Both are tough places of intense training, as many of us can probably verify from similar episodes in our own lives. One thing that will help us get through these painful times of shaping is to know and trust God's heart. Arthur T. Pierson captures it well:

> Being determined to perfect His saints, He puts His precious metal into His crucible. But He sits by it,

and watches it. Love is His thermometer, and marks the exact degree of heat; not one instant's unnecessary pang will He permit; and as soon as the dross is released so that He sees Himself reflected in the fire, the trial ceases.[5]

Remember, precious saint of His, love is always His thermometer.

🍇 Living Insights

Elijah left the dry boot camp of Cherith hoping to find something better at Zarephath. But what was the first scene to greet him? The person God had appointed to provide for him—a poor, starving widow who had given up hope and was ready to die. Talk about first-impression blues!

Just about every member of the human race can identify with this first test Elijah encountered. New schools, new jobs, new homes, new churches—all of them represent one of the toughest experiences life holds for us: beginnings. How well do you handle beginnings?

In the space provided, write down one new situation you have encountered. It may range from tackling a new task at work to forming a new friendship, something big or something small.

What was your first impression? Don't be shy now; write down your true feelings and thoughts.

What effect has your first impression had on you? Have you stalled in the doldrums of fear? Have you taken another tack? Have you hoisted your sails to meet the winds head-on?

---

5. Arthur T. Pierson, as quoted by Richard H. Seume in *Shoes for the Road* (Chicago, Ill.: Moody Press, 1974), p. 91.

Elijah was able to pass his test with flying colors because he trusted God more than his first impression—and because he didn't quit before he really got started. His example is one to follow, and so are the words of the philosopher Epictetus:

> Be not swept off your feet by the vividness of the impression, but say, "Impression, wait for me a little. Let me see what you are and what you represent. Let me try you."[6]

Or in the words of another wise man, "Trust in the Lord with all your heart, / And do not lean on your own understanding" (Prov. 3:5). Sound advice, especially when it comes to first impressions.

🍇 Living Insights

> "Arise, go to Zarephath, which belongs to Sidon, and stay there; behold, I have commanded a widow there to provide for you." . . . The bowl of flour was not exhausted nor did the jar of oil become empty, according to the word of the Lord. (1 Kings 17:9, 16a)

In His faithfulness, God provided not only for Elijah but also for the widow and her son. Now He didn't replenish the bowl with an unending supply of filet mignon, or keep filling the jar with an ever-flowing fountain of chocolate; He gave them just flour and oil. Just what they needed.

How has God provided for you? List four needs you know He has met, no matter if they were met with just flour and oil.

_____   _____

_____   _____

Have you received His provision with a grateful heart? Or have you been disappointed that He didn't give you more? Take some time to go into depth here, examining the reasons for your response.

_____

_____

6. Epictetus, as quoted in Bartlett's Familiar Quotations, 15th ed., rev. and enl., ed. Emily Morison Beck (Boston, Mass.: Little, Brown and Co., 1980), p. 121.

_____

_____

_____

_____

_____

Gratitude flows from hearts that are humble, that can recognize love when it's coming their way, that realize the gift in being given something. In short, "Gratitude is the memory of the heart."[7]

Why not make a grateful heart one of your life's priorities? Start by spending a week meditating on Psalm 103. Drink in what the psalmist says, then pour forth your own life into the psalm's mold. Soon you will be able to say with David, "Bless the Lord, O my soul"—even for flour and oil!

7. Jean Baptiste Massieu, as quoted in *The Home Book of Quotations*, 10th ed., comp. Burton Stevenson (New York, N.Y.: Dodd, Mead and Co., 1967), p. 823.

Chapter 4

A MIRACLE IN THE HOME

1 Kings 17:17–24

> "Great faith is not the faith that walks always in the light
> and knows no darkness, but the faith that perseveres in
> spite of God's seeming silences, and that faith will most
> certainly and surely get its reward."[1]

Scripture is replete with men and women who incarnated great
faith, who modeled it in their generation and model it still
today. For many of them, Hebrews 11 is their roll of honor—an
encapsulation of both the darknesses they faced and the sure rewards
they received. Consider their testimonies as their names ring out:

- "By faith Abel offered to God a better sacrifice
  than Cain, through which he obtained the testi-
  mony that he was righteous." (v. 4)

- "By faith Enoch was taken up so that he should
  not see death." (v. 5)

- "By faith Noah, being warned by God about
  things not yet seen, in reverence prepared an
  ark for the salvation of his household." (v. 7)

- "By faith Abraham, when he was called, obeyed
  by going out to a place which he was to receive
  for an inheritance; and he went out, not knowing where he was going." (v. 8)

- "By faith even Sarah herself received ability to
  conceive, even beyond the proper time of life."
  (v. 11)

- "By faith Moses, when he had grown up, refused
  to be called the son of Pharaoh's daughter; . . .
  considering the reproach of Christ greater riches
  than the treasures of Egypt." (vv. 24, 26)

---

1. Father Andrew, as quoted in *The Harper Religious and Inspirational Quotation Companion*,
comp. Margaret Pepper (New York, N.Y.: Harper and Row, Publishers, 1989), p. 172.

- "By faith Rahab the harlot did not perish along with those who were disobedient." (v. 31)

Out of breath, the inspired chronicler then asks, "And what more shall I say?" (v. 32a). For time would indeed fail us all if every person and act of faith were listed, from David to the prophets, from the shutting of lions' mouths to women receiving back their dead by resurrection (vv. 32b–35a).[2]

But one more person of great faith needs to be listed, and that's Elijah. For his faith will pass through the crucible of Zarephath at its hottest point. Here he will have to trust God to do something never before recorded: raise someone from the dead. And it's not just any someone, but the son of the impoverished widow he has been boarding with.

Context and Atmosphere

Our story opens with the words, "Now it came about after these things" (1 Kings 17:17a). In order to fully appreciate what an impact this episode will have on Elijah's life, we must remember what "these things" were.

The first of "these things" was his withering confrontation with Ahab, where Elijah prophesied unrelenting drought for "these years, except by my word" (v. 1).

Next was the beginning of Elijah's time in hiding, and of testing, which started at Cherith. Here the prophet's isolation was broken only by the cawing of the ravens, upon whom he was utterly dependent for his food. Then the brook, his only source of water, dried up.

From there Elijah came to Zarephath, where God said he was to be provided for by a widow. Any pride he had would have been melted here, as he humbly looked to this vulnerable woman to take care of his needs. But she was more than vulnerable; she was starving, ready to prepare the last meal for her son and herself. Elijah, however, knew God would keep His word; and He did, by providing both Elijah and the widow's family with a miraculously unending supply of flour and oil.

---

2. *Resurrection*, in this context, refers to a resuscitation of life. This occurs when a person comes back to life with the same body. *Resurrection*, technically, refers to a new life with a new body. See Charles C. Ryrie, *Basic Theology* (Wheaton, Ill.: Scripture Press Publications, Victor Books, 1986), pp. 517–22.

So it is in the context of "these things," and in the atmosphere of hiding, that Elijah will face yet another test—perhaps his greatest test of all.

Sickness and Death

Safe, fed, maybe even enjoying this taste of family life, Elijah is suddenly jolted out of Zarephath's comfortable routine by a grievous event.

> Now it came about after these things, that the son of the woman, the mistress of the house, became sick; and his sickness was so severe, that there was no breath left in him. (v. 17)

The Hebrew word for *breath* here, *neshamah*, is the same word used in Genesis 2:7, where the Lord created Adam and "breathed into his nostrils the breath of life." So 1 Kings 17:17 is not describing a respiratory ailment; it is telling us that the boy was no longer breathing. It is telling us that the only family, the only loved one the widow has left, is dead.

Who can fathom the agony of losing a child?

> Of all deaths, that of a child is most unnatural and hardest to bear.
> In Carl Jung's words, it is "a period placed before the end of the sentence," sometimes when the sentence has hardly begun.
> We expect the old to die. The separation is always difficult, but it comes as no surprise.
> But the child, the youth? Life lies ahead, with its beauty, its wonder, its potential. Death is a cruel thief when it strikes down the young.[3]

The widow, already bereft of her husband, now reels with this fresh loss. Her future, her plans, her dreams—all embodied in her tender little boy—lay spent and lifeless in her desperate arms. In her anguish and rage at this cruel thief, she strikes out at the only person near to her, Elijah.

---

3. Joseph Bayly, *The Last Thing We Talk About*, rev. ed. (Elgin, Ill.: David C. Cook Publishing Co., 1973), p. 65. The author lost three sons; one at eighteen days, after surgery; another at five years, from leukemia; and the third at eighteen years, after a sledding accident complicated by mild hemophilia (p. 66).

"What do I have to do with you, O man of God?
You have come to me to bring my iniquity to remem-
brance, and to put my son to death!" (v. 18)

Into her shattered heart a dark intruder comes . . . guilt. We've
no idea what her iniquity was, but in her mind it is enough to kill
her son. This thought, however, is too painful for her to face, so
she blames Elijah. Thus Elijah, the righteous man of God, becomes
in her mind Elijah, God's emissary of judgment. And before this
God of judgment, the widow feels utterly, hopelessly condemned.

Faith and Prayer

Looking at her tear-streaked face and eyes frantic with grief,
Elijah sees beyond her anger and is moved with compassion. Rather
than arguing with her or defending himself, he stands with her—
bearing the weight of her pain in a gentle, eloquent silence. A
silence that will be broken only by simple words of faith.

And he said to her, "Give me your son." Then he
took him from her bosom and carried him up to the
upper room where he was living, and laid him on
his own bed. (v. 19)

As the widow had cradled her boy in her arms, so Elijah now
cradles her heart in his. He gets alone with God, gets to a protected
place where he can pour out his heart and search God's mercy. And
he takes the risk of getting deeply, personally involved in her need.

And he called to the Lord and said, "O Lord my
God, hast Thou also brought calamity to the widow
with whom I am staying, by causing her son to die?"
Then he stretched himself upon the child three times,
and called to the Lord, and said, "O Lord my God,
I pray Thee, let this child's life return to him."
(vv. 20–21)

Once . . . twice . . . three times Elijah stretches himself upon
the boy—body to body, arm to arm, leg to leg. It's as if Elijah
somehow thinks that a transfusion of life could occur under this
canopy of contact. But Elijah is stretched in more than body; his
very faith strains for a miracle never before performed, reaches for
a mercy God has never before bestowed.

And God grasps His servant's outstretched hand.

Miracle and Praise

Sweat beading on his forehead, Elijah holds his breath and watches the boy intently. Was that his eyelid fluttering? Did his finger really twitch? Oh, how gracious and kind the Lord is!

> And the Lord heard the voice of Elijah, and the life
> of the child returned to him and he revived. (v. 22)

Panting, laughing, praising God, Elijah helps the boy sit up. The boy's small, pallid face brightens with a sunrise glow. His listless eyes dance with the light of life again. And Elijah's heart fills with grateful joy—a joy he can hardly wait to give to a certain mother.

> And Elijah took the child, and brought him down
> from the upper room into the house and gave him
> to his mother; and Elijah said, "See, your son is
> alive." (v. 23)

No "Ta da!" No "I told you I was a man of God." No "Look what I have done!" Just a tender "See, your son is alive." See, God is alive, powerful, caring, and kind. See, He, not Baal, is the one and only true God. And as her burning tears of sorrow ebb, her eyes clear . . . and she sees.

> Then the woman said to Elijah, "Now I know that
> you are a man of God, and that the word of the
> Lord in your mouth is truth." (v. 24)

Concluding Applications

"Now I know that you are a man of God," the widow said, because she saw Elijah's faith and the power of God working through him.

How can we be like Elijah? How can we, too, be people of great faith? We can examine how Elijah demonstrated his faith during this time of training at Zarephath. At least four of his inner attitudes stand out.

First: *He demonstrated calmness and contentment.* Not a word of complaint fell from his lips about his accommodations or his food— items that generally agitate us if they are not just right.

Second: *He demonstrated gentleness and self-control.* When the widow lashed out at Elijah in her searing grief, he remained silent until he knew what to do. And then, gently, he lifted her burden from her and took it for his own, presenting the concern to God.

Third: *He demonstrated undiminished faith.* Elijah stretched himself out in prayer again and again until he received an answer. Had God said no, he would have known and stopped; but he felt the Lord's Spirit heavy upon him to intercede for the boy. Such sensitivity to the Lord comes from an intimate knowledge of God and is learned by trusting Him through many Cherith and Zarephath experiences.

Fourth: *He demonstrated humility.* When God displayed His power, Elijah gave Him center stage; he stood in the wings and listened to the applause that was not for himself but for God's merciful and mighty work. Elijah's humility came from realizing that he had been allowed to be a part of something beyond himself, beyond what he could have ever dreamed.

All over this world, there are "widows"—the broken, the needy, the hurting—who are hungry and crying out for God's presence. They don't need indignant arguing or defensive declarations against the questions that spring from their anguish; they just need to feel the touch of God's care. So—in gentleness and humility, in seeking God and risking opening our hearts to involvement—this is where great faith is demonstrated. This is how we can be like Elijah.

🍇 *Living Insights* STUDY ONE

What do you say to someone who is grieving? It is a difficult question, because there are no formulas, no "if such-and-such happens, use response A; if this-or-that occurs, use response B.

A father who lost his twenty-five-year-old son in a climbing accident reflects:

> Some people are gifted with words of wisdom. For such, one is profoundly grateful. . . . But not all are gifted in that way.[4]

Elijah, perhaps, was one of those who are not gifted that way. So he kept still . . . he kept the widow safe from any further hurt

---

4. Nicholas Wolterstorff, *Lament for a Son* (Grand Rapids, Mich.: William B. Eerdmans Publishing Co., 1987), p. 34.

that could have been inflicted by untimely words. And perhaps the widow heard the unspoken words of his heart—why else would she have let him take her son?

> The heart that speaks is heard more than the words spoken. And if you can't think of anything at all to say, just say, "I can't think of anything to say. But I want you to know that we are with you in your grief."[5]

"I am with you in your grief," Elijah's heart seemed to say. He didn't turn away nor promise not to intrude on her privacy. He came close, took her burden out of her arms and into his, joined her before God in her suffering.

He did what the twenty-year-old son's father longed for.

> If you think your task as comforter is to tell me that really, all things considered, it's not so bad, you do not sit with me in my grief but place yourself off in the distance away from me. Over there, you are of no help. What I need to hear from you is that you recognize how painful it is. I need to hear from you that you are with me in my desperation. To comfort me, you have to come close. Come sit beside me on my mourning bench.[6]

Close and quiet—but not stoic. Elijah did not sit stiffly on the widow's mourning bench; he stretched himself over her pain three times, calling out to God all the while. Elijah's empathy is illustrated by a father and his dying son. This father observed well-meaning friends who failed to understand the need to express their own grief toward the suffering.

> Some . . . fear they will break down. So they put on a brave face and lid their feelings—never reflecting, I suppose, that this adds new pain to the sorrow of their suffering friends. Your tears are salve on our wound.[7]

5. Wolterstorff, *Lament for a Son*, p. 34.

6. Wolterstorff, *Lament for a Son*, p. 34.

7. Wolterstorff, *Lament for a Son*, p. 35.

◆

As you reflect on this father's words, do you feel fear knotting in your stomach? Anxiety pounding through your heart? Drawing near to someone in the intensity of grief can be frightening. Not because the person is scary, but because you don't want to do anything that would add to the already engulfing levels of pain—and, maybe, because not knowing what to do is in itself such a helpless, awkward feeling.

It is our hope that Elijah's example and this father's words will give you a start in learning what you *can* do to help those who grieve. To help you further, here are a few more ideas.

- Learn about the grieving process. See Cyril J. Barber's and Sharalee Aspenleiter's *Through the Valley of Tears* (Old Tappan, N.J.: Fleming H. Revell Co., 1987) and Joseph Bayly's *The Last Thing We Talk About* (Elgin, Ill.: David C. Cook Publishing Co., 1973).

- Read about how grief and sorrow feel so that you can better understand your suffering friend's feelings. See Nicholas Wolterstorff's *Lament for a Son* (Grand Rapids, Mich.: William B. Eerdmans Co., 1987), C. S. Lewis' *A Grief Observed* (San Francisco, Calif.: Harper and Row, Publishers, 1961), and any other book describing personal experience with grief.

- Get some instruction on how to comfort. Try Warren W. and David W. Wiersbe's *Comforting the Bereaved* (Chicago, Ill.: Moody Press, 1985) and Katie Maxwell's *Bedside Manners* (Grand Rapids, Mich.: Baker Book House, 1990) for starters.

- Find out how Christ responded to grief by meditating on John 11.

And remember, unlike this widow's experience, most grief doesn't end in a day.

> And later, when you ask me how I am doing and
> I respond with a quick, thoughtless "Fine" or "OK,"
> stop me sometime and ask, "No, I mean *really*."[8]

---

8. Wolterstorff, *Lament for a Son*, p. 35.

A widow walks to her son's bedroom, and there she sees him sleeping so quiet, so still. Watching him, she becomes concerned, then frightened. She touches him and a damp coldness replies, causing her to quickly withdraw her hand in shock. Then, frantically, she embraces him and tries to awaken him, but to no avail. All breath, all warmth, all life has fled from him.

Why? Oh, God, why? she wonders in her heart. And as she gropes for an answer in the darkness of her pain, guilt slips out of the shadows it has been lurking in and attacks.

"Why? I'll tell you why—because of you, because of your sins. God has taken your boy to give you the punishment you deserve!"

Writhing at this new thought, she screams out at God's man,

> "What do I have to do with you, O man of God?
> You have come to me to bring my iniquity to remembrance, and to put my son to death!" (1 Kings 17:18)

Guilt. The woman is not free from her past; the memories still have the power to torment her.[9]

When tragedy strikes you, does guilt attack you too? What kind of thoughts and accusations come stabbing at your heart? Bring them out of the shadows and into the light by writing them down.

———————————————————————————

———————————————————————————

———————————————————————————

What do you feel God is thinking of you during these times of tragedy? Do you believe He hates you, that everyone else is eligible for His love and forgiveness but you? Be honest here.

———————————————————————————

———————————————————————————

———————————————————————————

9. A word must be said here about false guilt. False guilt comes when you live under other people's expectations and fail—you develop feelings of shame when you are reminded repeatedly of your inability to perform at a level of peer or parental expectations. A wise person studies to distinguish between cultural and godly standards. A good resource to begin with is Earl D. Wilson's book *Counseling and Guilt*, vol. 8 of *Resources for Christian Counseling*, ed. Gary R. Collins (Waco, Tex.: Word Books, 1987).

In order to protect yourself from the lies and attacks that guilt can mount against you, you need to have a clear understanding of God's heart . . . because He is *so* ready and willing to respond to your cry for forgiveness and cleansing. Just read 1 John 1:9. Exactly what is required to deal with known sin?

So, He is faithful and righteous—true to His Word—to forgive and cleanse you completely. Still not sure? Then immerse yourself in the living waters of Psalm 103:12–14 and Romans 8:1, 33–34. And when painful circumstances come knocking, bringing along the specters of sins past, remember that you are forgiven, and let Christ open that door.

Chapter 5

THE GOD WHO
ANSWERS BY FIRE

1 Kings 18:1–2, 17–40

P rove it!" As trust and confidence wane in our society, "prove it" has become a wary catch phrase—not only between people, but between us and God. Many demand God to *prove* His existence to their satisfaction before they will commit to Him, all the while ignoring the everyday evidence right in front of their noses (see Rom. 1:20; Ps. 19:1–4a). Is this kind of stubborn blindness really unique to our age? Sadly, no; it's been with us since time began.

God never has been and never will be pleased when He is put to the test by us. But there are times when He will pull back the curtain and reveal Himself beyond doubt. And of all such events recorded in the Bible, one of the most spectacular "prove its" is found in 1 Kings 18.

For here we'll see Elijah, his life rooted in Israel's struggle with idolatry, confront his nation's need to return to their belief in God—which is close to zero. Elijah, just one man, will be God's courageous instrument of "proving it" to His people . . . by fire.

Events Leading to Carmel

Elijah's faith wasn't flamed to life in a vacuum . . . far from it. It was forged instead by times of testing and trials: facing off with Ahab on the subject of drought, camping out at Cherith, taking charity from a starving widow.

Now, however, his time of training is over. He's learned through experience that He can rely on God, and he's ready to reemerge into public ministry. And with his release comes relief from the drought.

> Now it came about after many days, that the word of the Lord came to Elijah in the third year, saying, "Go, show yourself to Ahab, and I will send rain on the face of the earth." So Elijah went to show himself to Ahab. Now the famine was severe in Samaria. (18:1–2)

According to his instructions, Elijah makes arrangements to get together with Ahab, and at the appointed time, he sets off to meet him. Ahab also makes his way to the fateful meeting—probably having to carefully wend his way through the rotting carcasses of drought-starved cattle. By this time he is convinced that Elijah is controlling the drought; and, as you can imagine, their encounter is not pleasant.

> And Ahab went to meet Elijah. And it came about, when Ahab saw Elijah that Ahab said to him, "Is this you, you troubler of Israel?" (vv. 16b–17)

But Elijah is not intimidated by royalty or anything else. He goes nose to nose with Ahab.

> "I have not troubled Israel, but you and your father's house have, because you have forsaken the commandments of the Lord, and you have followed the Baals." (v. 18)

In today's language, Elijah was saying, "You don't get it, do you, Ahab? *You* are the reason there has been no rain." Not one to back down, Elijah tells the king straight out why the stench of death is blowing across his country . . . and goes on to meet the challenge in Ahab's "prove it!" attitude. But the showdown won't be in private. He's going to expose Ahab's evil, powerless gods in front of all of Israel.

Preparation for the Proof

Elijah requests that the principal players be called to the arena.

Two Groups

> "Now then send and gather to me all Israel at Mount Carmel, together with 450 prophets of Baal and 400 prophets of the Asherah, who eat at Jezebel's table. (vv. 19–20)

Eight hundred and fifty false prophets pitted against Elijah . . . and at his own request! But Elijah knew he had Almighty God beside him as he strode up the mountain for the confrontation.

One Plan

With the prophets and the people in place, Elijah issues a challenge of decision to the Israelites.

"How long will you hesitate between two opinions? If the Lord is God, follow Him; but if Baal, follow him." But the people did not answer him a word. (v. 21)

While some in the crowd are hard-core Baal- and Asherah-worshipers, others surely feel a long-dormant stirring of the old days and faith in the God of heaven. But the idol shrines, like silent sentinels, stand menacingly by. To choose against these gods means condemnation, because it would be a swift backhand to the queen's religion. So Israel remains silent in the face of Elijah's concern.

Clearly, their silence needs to be shattered. And that's just what Elijah's going to do.

Presentation of the Proof

Elijah's spirit rises in spite of the people's mute apathy and their stone images, because *his* shrines are vivid mental images of Cherith and Zarephath, where God taught him of His sufficiency. He has the proof that God is God—experientially.

The Proposition

With his boot-camp days fresh in his memory, he makes them an offer they can't refuse.

"I alone am left a prophet of the Lord, but Baal's prophets are 450 men. Now let them give us two oxen; and let them choose one ox for themselves and cut it up, and place it on the wood, but put no fire under it; and I will prepare the other ox, and lay it on the wood, and I will not put a fire under it. Then you call on the name of your god, and I will call on the name of the Lord, and the God who answers by fire, He is God." And all the people answered and said, "That is a good idea." (vv. 22–24)

So the conditions of the test are set. The prophets of Baal will have their turn, followed by Elijah. And the people are intrigued.

The Prophets and Baal

As Elijah gives further instructions, you can feel the electricity in the air.

So Elijah said to the prophets of Baal, "Choose one ox for yourselves and prepare it first for you are many, and call on the name of your god, but put no fire under it." (v. 25)

So the prophets of Baal begin.

> Then they took the ox which was given them and they prepared it and called on the name of Baal from morning until noon saying, "O Baal, answer us." But there was no voice and no one answered. And they leaped about the altar which they made. (v. 26)

All morning they carry on their ritual while the people watch. No one leaves *this* scene. At noon Elijah begins to press these religious charlatans, playing on their fanaticism to heighten their frenzied activity.

> And it came about at noon, that Elijah mocked them and said, "Call out with a loud voice, for he is a god; either he is occupied or gone aside, or is on a journey, or perhaps he is asleep and needs to be awakened." (v. 27)

Aggravated by Elijah's sarcasm and Baal's silence, they desperately begin yelling louder and even slash their bodies to prove their sincerity.

> So they cried with a loud voice and cut themselves according to their custom with swords and lances until the blood gushed out on them. (v. 28)

On into midafternoon they howled, scratched, and screamed . . .

> but there was no voice, no one answered, and no one paid attention. (v. 29b)

Baal's prophets had failed.

The Prophet and Jehovah God

The camera shifts away from the exhausted priests and zooms in on Elijah. It's his turn now. Notice how his eyes flash confidence and expectation as he speaks.

> Then Elijah said to all the people, "Come near to me." So all the people came near to him. And he repaired the altar of the Lord which had been torn down . . . and he made a trench around the

41

altar, large enough to hold two measures of seed.
Then he arranged the wood and cut the ox in pieces
and laid it on the wood. (vv. 30, 32b–33a)

Calling for water—lots of it—he drenches everything, one,
two, three times.[1] And now he's ready.

Elijah's eyes scan the crowd. The dignitaries, the bleeding prophets . . . everyone is silent, anticipating what he will do.

He prays.

"O Lord, the God of Abraham, Isaac and Israel,
today let it be known that Thou art God in Israel,
and that I am Thy servant, and that I have done all
these things at Thy word." (v. 36b)

Elijah draws attention to Israel's ancient God as the author of
this event. His opening line recalls his people to their rich history,
though it is a mere whispering echo from the past. And as these
thoughts slip into their minds, Elijah finishes his prayer.

"Answer me, O Lord, answer me, that this people
may know that Thou, O Lord, art God, and that
Thou hast turned their heart back again." (v. 37)

What happens next is shocking because, by contrast to the false
prophets' experience, it is instantaneous and spectacular.

Then the fire of the Lord fell, and consumed the
burnt offering and the wood and the stones and the
dust, and licked up the water that was in the trench.
(v. 38)

A blinding flash, and POOF! Everything is reduced to fine ash,
including the stones. Wow!

Response to the Events at Carmel

As the smoke cleared, two responses were revealed—worship,
on the people's faces; and dread, on the faces of the prophets.

And when all the people saw it, they fell on their
faces; and they said, "The Lord, He is God; the
Lord, He is God." (v. 39)

1. Mount Carmel rises from the Great or Mediterranean Sea, making salt water readily available.

The pendulum of allegiance has swung to Elijah's God. And he wastes no time in calling them to act on their renewed faith.

> Then Elijah said to them, "Seize the prophets of Baal; do not let one of them escape." So they seized them; and Elijah brought them down to the brook Kishon, and slew them there. (v. 40)

An extreme response? No more than treating a malignant tumor with surgery. Likewise, when God diagnoses national cancer and chooses a surgeon to remove it, His methods have to be radical too. Avoiding such surgery could re-expose His people to a deadly spiritual sickness . . . from which they might never recover.

Four Lessons for Today

From our story it is crystal clear that God really cares whether our hearts are wholly His. As you seek to walk with God and give Him more and more of your heart, take these four lessons with you. They will guide and encourage you along the way.

First: *When we are sure we are in the will of God, we are invincible.* Even in the most threatening circumstances, if you are in the will of God, you need not be intimidated by anybody or anything. Though outnumbered, humanly speaking, Elijah shone with the confidence of having God on his side during his confrontation with Israel's idolatry.

Second: *Divided allegiance is as wrong as open idolatry.* The easiest thing to do when outnumbered is to assume a mediocre stance of noncommitment. But if you try to straddle a religious fence, as the Israelites did, you court the danger of falling off into idolatry. Elijah confronted religious apostasy, prodding his hearers to make a decision and get off that fence.

Third: *In the final analysis, our most effective tool is prayer.* In contrast with the methods of Baal's prophets, Elijah's prayer is stunningly simple and effective. He knew what God wanted from His people: that they acknowledge Him as God and turn back to Him. Could he get them to do this in his own power? No. So he didn't even try. Instead, his first course of action was prayer. And how God responded! Are you using the Christian's most effective tool? Or are you trying to rout all the false prophets empty-handed?

Fourth: *Never underestimate the power of one life totally dedicated to the Lord.* Elijah's arms, legs, and voice were totally dedicated to

God's purposes. Are yours? God works through frail people, like us, when our hearts are completely His.

Elijah's faith encourages us to live in a way that challenges others about the reality of God. Our task is to help them comprehend God's truth, feel His love, so much so that they, too, begin to seek Him.

🍇 Living Insights

> What comes into our minds when we think about God is the most important thing about us. . . .
>
> All the problems of heaven and earth . . . would be nothing compared with the overwhelming problem of God: That He *is*; what He is *like*; and what we as moral beings must *do* about Him.[2]

What comes into your mind when you think about God? Elijah knew Him as the mighty God of Abraham, Isaac, and Jacob, the God of history and the future. No wonder he could stand so fearlessly before Ahab, nearly a thousand hostile false prophets, and an entire nation of apathetic backsliders!

In order to be able to stand as Elijah did, we need to have a solid resting place for our faith. And the best place is on one of God's names. So let's set aside some time right now to study a name that will encourage your confidence and joy in Him—*Jehovah Roi*, or "the Lord is my Shepherd."

Read Psalm 23, and, through the window of the biblical text, view how God shepherds your life. Read the passage written below; and below each, write a few words that indicate the ways God takes care of His sheep.

Example: He makes me lie down in green pastures (v. 2a)

Meaning: *He gives us rest*

He leads me beside quiet waters (v. 2b)

Meaning: _____

---

2. A. W. Tozer, *The Knowledge of the Holy* (New York, N.Y.: Harper and Row, Publishers, 1961), pp. 9–10.

He restores my soul (v. 3a)

Meaning: _____

He guides me in the paths of righteousness (v. 3b)

Meaning: _____

Even though I walk through the valley of the shadow of death, I fear no evil; for Thou art with me (v. 4)

Meaning: _____

Thou dost prepare a table before me (v. 5a)

Meaning: _____

In the presence of my enemies (v. 5a)

Meaning: _____

Thou hast anointed my head with oil (v. 5b)

Meaning: _____

Surely goodness and lovingkindness will follow me all the days of my life (v. 6a)

Meaning: _____

Which aspect of God's shepherding is most meaningful to you? Why? _____

_____

_____

_____

_____

What kind of effects will remembering this name have in your life?

_____

_____

_____

_____

How is God's existence demonstrated today? How can we, as His people, respond effectively to the "prove it" challenge? We can't call fire down from heaven like Elijah did, but we can light the candle that illumines the answer: *unity*.

When united with people from all ethnic, social, and economic backgrounds, we draw attention to His supernatural unity. Because unity is one of God's hallmarks.

> "And the glory which Thou hast given Me I have given to them; that they may be one, just as We are one. I in them, and Thou in Me, that they may be perfected in unity, that the world may know that Thou didst send Me, and didst love them, even as Thou didst love Me." (John 17:22–23)

Something wonderful is revealed when social, economic, and ethnic barriers are broken down—people just don't normally overcome such diverse backgrounds and interests. But God's people do. And when we come together, we reveal God's all-conquering love. A love that "proves it" to a watching world.

So let's probe our response to God's love and how we contribute to Christian unity. Questions have a way of nudging us, like this one: Have others ever commented on your ability to involve yourself with all kinds of people—regardless of their social status? Check the box that best represents your answer.

Never ☐   Occasionally ☐   Frequently ☐

Explain your answer.

_____

_____

_____

Now think carefully about C. S. Lewis' words about a person's splendor—or horror—in the afterlife.

> The load . . . of my neighbor's glory should be laid on my back, a load so heavy that only humility can carry it, and the backs of the proud will be broken. It is a serious thing . . . to remember that the dullest and most uninteresting person you can talk to

may one day be a creature which . . . you would be strongly tempted to worship, or else a horror and a corruption such as you now meet, if at all, only in a nightmare. All day long we are, in some degree, helping each other to one or other of these destinations. . . . It is with the awe and the circumspection proper to them, that we should conduct all our dealings with one another, all friendships, all loves, all play, all politics. There are no *ordinary people*.[3]

God understands better than any of us: All people are *extraordinary*. Which is why God's "prove it" rests in His infinite love being passed along from us to others.

3. C. S. Lewis, *The Weight of Glory and Other Addresses*, rev. and exp. (New York, N.Y.: Macmillan Publishing Co., 1980), pp. 18–19.

Chapter 6

KNEELING ON THE PROMISES

1 Kings 18:41–46

In the early nineteenth century, George Müller went to his knees, claiming God's promise that He would be a "Father to the fatherless" (Ps. 68:5). He prayed that God would provide food and supplies for an orphanage under his care, and God graciously responded to their needs. As his prayer relationship with the Father deepened, Müller learned much about the nature of praying. He passed on his counsel to future generations through his writings.

> It is not enough to begin to pray, nor to pray aright; nor is it enough to continue *for a time* to pray—but we must patiently, believingly continue in prayer . . . *to continue* in prayer unto the end, but we have also *to believe* that God does hear us and will answer our prayers. Most frequently we fail *in not continuing* in prayer until the blessing is obtained, and *in not expecting* the blessing.[1]

Thousands of years earlier, another man prayed. Not for food, but for rain after 3½ years of drought. That man was Elijah. God had promised to send rain, and Elijah was cashing in that promise . . . but before we go any further in Elijah's story, let's make a detour to the subject of promises.

God's Promises to Us: Clarification

The Bible is chock-full of promises, everything from the ten plagues to salvation. But are all those promises meant for us? Could a drought-plagued farmer claim God's promise to Elijah and expect it to rain on his fields? Does it really work to open your Bible and randomly stab your finger on a verse, hoping to discover God's direction? How can we know which of God's promises to claim? We can do this by keeping in mind the following two guidelines.

---

1. Frederick G. Warne, *George Müller: The Modern Apostle of Faith*, 7th ed. (London, England: S. W. Partridge and Co., 1911), pp. 197–98.

First: *Some promises are universal, while others are personal.* Universal promises apply to every believer. One example would be Matthew 11:28: "Come to Me, all who are weary and heavy-laden, and I will give you rest." Promises made to individuals, on the other hand, are meant for them alone. For example, God promised Joshua that if he marched around Jericho seven times, he would conquer the city (Josh. 6:2–5). Today, any general who would deploy his troops in such a way would invite embarrassment; we know intuitively that God did not intend this as a universal military strategy. In light of this, we should avoid claiming Bible promises made to specific individuals.

Next: *Some promises are conditional.* These will be fulfilled by God only if you have done your part. For example,

> If we confess our sins, He is faithful and righteous
> to forgive us our sins and to cleanse us from all
> unrighteousness. (1 John 1:9)

The "if" indicates our part. *If* your hearts acknowledge known sin, *then* God will bathe us in His forgiveness. It's important to check whether we have a part to fulfill before expecting God to act as He promised.

With these principles in mind, let's go on to find out how prayer plays a role in this next installment of Elijah's story.

God's Promise to Elijah: Exposition

Elijah's promise from God was both personal *and* conditional; therefore, it cannot be claimed universally. It was made to him exclusively, but it had a certain condition he had to fulfill.

The Promise Declared

> Now it came about after many days, that the
> word of the Lord came to Elijah in the third year,
> saying, "Go, show yourself to Ahab, and I will send
> rain on the face of the earth." (1 Kings 18:1)

When God said, "Go, show yourself to Ahab," that meant that Elijah had to first obey before God would release rain to satisfy the parched soil's thirst.

And Elijah did obey. He confronted Ahab and all the false prophets, with simple but fervent prayer. And in one blinding moment, fire from God fell and consumed the entire altar—and all the people knew who the real God was (vv. 16–39). Elijah has finished his part. *Now* it's time for rain—this is God's part.

Elijah's next words to the stunned and spiritually defeated Ahab reveal the prophet's unwavering trust in God.

> Now Elijah said to Ahab, "Go up, eat and drink;
> for there is the sound of the roar of a heavy shower."
> (v. 41)

Does this mean he heard thunder? Or that his hearing was so acute that he could hear rain in the distance? No, there's no scriptural evidence for a gift like that. Rather, Elijah's confidence in God is so real that he hears the sound of promised rain with ears of faith. And his heart and mind are flooded with rain, though the skies across the horizon, as far as he can see, are cloudless.

The Promise Claimed

With Ahab dispatched, Elijah moves up the slope of the region's sentinel, Mount Carmel (v. 42a). Once at the top, he again comes before God in prayer. From his example, we can learn several principles for communicating with God.

First: *Elijah separated himself.* He climbs a mountaintop to do business with God. Now, we don't need a mountain in order to isolate ourselves; a bedroom, a closet, a car, or a solitary walk or run would do just as well. Why is this privacy so important? Because it sequesters us with our own thoughts; it frees us from distraction so that we can listen for God's voice. This is where the discipline of prayer begins.

Second: *Elijah humbled himself.*

> And he crouched down on the earth, and put his
> face between his knees. (v. 42b)

Elijah's posture shows that he doesn't approach his Lord arrogantly, but with utter humility. This is all the more striking when you remember that he has just single-handedly subdued Jezebel's hundreds of religious advisors. Close on the heels of victory, his spirit could have been proudly exulting in the achievement. But instead, he drops his head between his knees and is humble before God.

Third: *Elijah was confident and specific.* This aspect of his prayer life is revealed in his words to the servant who accompanied him:

> "Go up now, look toward the sea." (v. 43a)

Elijah has prayed so specifically and so confidently for rain that he has no doubt of what his servant will see—storm clouds gathering on the horizon. He had done what God had asked; now he was absolutely certain that God would do as He had promised.

When you pray, are you specific? God loves to answer specific requests—whatever weighs upon your heart. Be confident; your Father cares.

Fourth: *Elijah was persistent and fervent.* With his servant's eyes trained on the sea, Elijah waits for a sign of the fulfillment of God's promise. But his servant only said,

> "There is nothing." And [Elijah] said, "Go back" seven times. (v. 43b)

With the widow's boy, Elijah prayed three times. But here he prays for awhile and then sends his helper not just three times, but four, five, six, *seven* times. No doubt he would have kept at it for as long as necessary to accomplish his request.

How do you handle it when answers to prayer don't come immediately? Do you give up? Does your faith waiver? Waiting is hard work, a test designed to keep us fervently and persistently trusting. Elijah tenaciously hung onto God's promise. And because he was confident that God would keep His word, he patiently kept on praying and waiting, because he knew God would deliver His part of the promise. Take a lesson from Elijah in fervent prayer.

Fifth: *Elijah was expectant.* Finally, his servant returns with some good news.

> And it came about at the seventh time, that he said, "Behold, a cloud as small as a man's hand is coming up from the sea." (v. 44a)

There it is, a hand-sized cloud rising from the Mediterranean Sea—the portent of a magnificent storm! Despite the cloud's smallness, Elijah expectantly tells his servant to

> "Go up, say to Ahab, 'Prepare your chariot and go down, so that the heavy shower does not stop you.'" (v. 44b)

Visually, all Elijah had to go by was a little cloud . . . but in his heart he had the promise of God.

The Promise Fulfilled

The small cloud gathers moisture, and the wind begins to blow.

More clouds form, and daylight disappears behind these mammoth mountains of darkness in the sky.

> So it came about in a little while, that the sky grew black with clouds and wind, and there was a heavy shower. And Ahab rode and went to Jezreel. (v. 45)

Jezreel, probably Ahab's summer residence, is about twenty miles west of Mount Carmel. And Ahab is on his way there in his chariot. But Elijah?

> Then the hand of the Lord was on Elijah, and he girded up his loins and outran Ahab to Jezreel. (v. 46)

Ahab probably thinks, "Whaaaat?" He must have craned his neck, gaping in astonishment as Elijah streaked past him. "This man is something else. First he tells me there will be no rain. And no rain falls for 3½ years. After that he tells me to get up the mountain, and his God visits us with fire. He kills all my wife's priests and prophets, and then he tells me to hightail it to Jezreel. And there he goes, running faster than my horses and chariot! Jezebel won't believe this."

Elijah must haved seemed like a god himself. But he wasn't. His power didn't lie in himself; rather, "the hand of the Lord" was on him (v. 46a). He was a man, a *mere* man, dedicated to the Lord (see James 5:17–18).

God's Promises Today: Application

From Elijah's prayer life we can glean at least two lessons to apply to our own prayer time with God.

Prayer is exciting, but it is never glamorous. It is easier to study prayer and watch it in the life of another than to actually be consistent in its practice. Knee ministry sometimes means grappling with God on behalf of His people. Exciting, yes; but never glamorous.

Promises are available, but they're not automatic. Grab your mining gear and dig into God's Word to find those promises that are applicable to you. To help you discover them, read on to the two Living Insights.

An effective prayer life involves four phases—stages that require diligence, but will result in growth. Let's explore each of these phases in some depth, personalizing and applying them so that our prayers will come alive.

First, *finding the promise*. This is the discovery stage, where you learn which promises apply to you and what conditions they might entail. The best place to find God's promises are in God's Word—and the more consistent your time in the Bible, the more promises you're likely to find. It doesn't matter too much where you begin; God's promises are too numerous to count.

Once you've located a promise, read the context surrounding it carefully. Is it a universal promise, applicable to anyone; or a personal promise, meant only for that individual at a certain time in a particular situation? After taking time to determine this, read the passage again. Are any conditions attached to that promise? If so, what are they?

To get a feel for this process, let's use Matthew 11:28 as an example.

1. Is it universal or personal? Explain your reasoning.

_____

_____

2. What, if any, are the conditions?

_____

_____

Second, *claiming the promise*. This is the praying stage, where you personalize—own—the promise, and deal with the specifics of your situation. This is also the time to address any conditional aspects of it.

Using Matthew 11:28–30 as an example, what actions do you need to take to fulfill your part of the promise? Remember to check out the context!

_____

_____

Before you claim the promise of rest, what characteristics of Christ should you embrace?

_____

_____

Now, ask Him, in prayer, to establish these qualities in your life.

> Praying must come out of a cleansed heart and be presented and urged with the "lifting up of holy hands." It must be fortified by a life aiming, unceasingly, to obey God, to attain conformity to the Divine law, and to come into submission to the Divine will.[2]

Remember, learning to kneel on the promises takes time and effort—lots of it. It may help to set up some goals that will assist you to complete your part in the promise.

In the next Living Insight, we'll dig into the two final phases of praying through promises.

🍇 *Living Insights* STUDY TWO

Stages three and four complete the process.

Third, *resting in the promise*. This is the waiting stage. As a loving parent, God knows what timing is best for you. Perhaps He just wants to strengthen your trust in Him by stretching you. This is not to be confused with some who say that if you don't hear from God it is because you are lacking in faith. However, this is not the issue here; rather, it is personal growth and development. While you wait, trust your Father's heart; resist the temptation to go ahead of Him.

> Therefore the Lord longs to be gracious to you,
> And therefore He waits on high to have compassion
> on you.
> For the Lord is a God of justice;
> How blessed are all those who long for Him.
> (Isa. 30:18)

2. E. M. Bounds, *The Necessity of Prayer* (Grand Rapids, Mich.: Baker Book House, 1976), p. 88.

Fourth, *experiencing the promise.* This is the results stage. God's answer may come to you in a matter of minutes, or it may take years. Looking back over your life, what are some answers you have received from the Lord as a result of something He promised in the Bible?

_____

_____

Describe your feeling when you received what God had promised.

_____

_____

One day we will all shout, "Worthy is the Lamb that was slain" (Rev. 5:12)—in acknowledgment of Jesus' rightful place not only as Lord of all creation, but also as Redeemer . . . as the One who ripped away the dark barrier between us and God. Let's accept His invitation to enter boldly into His presence—without apology—and seek the necessary grace to meet our needs (Heb. 4:16)!

Chapter 7

SURE CURE FOR THE BLUES

1 Kings 19:1–18, 21

The blues—who, even among Christians, hasn't struggled with them? Charles Haddon Spurgeon, the great nineteenth-century preacher, found that even spiritual leaders are susceptible. He called their down times "the minister's fainting fits."

> Fits of depression come over the most of us. . . . The strong are not always vigorous, the wise not always ready, the brave not always courageous, and the joyous not always happy. . . .
>   . . . Such was my experience when I first became a pastor in London. My success appalled me; and the thought of the career which it seemed to open up, so far from elating me, cast me into the lowest depth. . . . Who was I that I should continue to lead so great a multitude?[1]

These same words could have been spoken by many great biblical leaders as well. Moses, for instance, gave up and asked God to kill him, even though he was leading thousands through the wilderness (Num. 11). Jonah was also ready to curl up and die after a wonderfully successful revival at Nineveh (Jon. 4). And even the great apostle Paul confessed that he "despaired even of life" while ministering in Asia (2 Cor. 1).

But another great minister of old who experienced a "fainting fit" may surprise you—the prophet Elijah. Grappling for his life with the devil Despair, he also entered depression's darkness. How could this happen to our man who has been so tested and found so true? Perhaps boot camp doesn't prepare one for everything.

This chapter is an adaptation of "The Prophet Who Prayed to Die," from the study guide *Great Stories from Old Testament Lives*, coauthored by Bryce Klabunde, from the Bible-teaching ministry of Charles R. Swindoll (Anaheim, Calif.: Insight for Living, 1992).

1. C. H. Spurgeon, *Lectures to My Students* (reprint, Grand Rapids, Mich.: Associated Publishers and Authors, 1971), pp. 167, 173.

The Setting of the Story

Four personalities play key roles in this story of Elijah's blues and his recovery: Ahab, Jezebel, Elijah, and the Lord.

The Henpecked Husband (Ahab)

Frightened and worried after the events on Carmel, Ahab scurried home to "Mama"—his wife, Jezebel—and tattled on Elijah, the meanie who had embarrassed him and destroyed all their prophets (1 Kings 19:1). Like many husbands who are controlled by domineering wives, he fell apart under pressure, reverting to the role of a child.

The Domineering Wife (Jezebel)

While soothing her little man, Jezebel boiled with anger against Elijah. Turning quickly to Ahab's defense, she took matters into her own hands and issued an edict.

> Then Jezebel sent a messenger to Elijah, saying, "So may the gods do to me and even more, if I do not make your life as the life of one of them by tomorrow about this time." (v. 2)

The Defeated Prophet (Elijah)

And what is Elijah's response? He had just faced an entire nation who opposed him; he had personally executed the 450 prophets of Baal (18:40); and he had prayed for rain on a cloudless day, and torrents had flooded the earth. He had even raced Ahab, who was in a chariot, back to Jezreel and won—on foot (vv. 45–46)! You'd think Elijah would have been standing on a mountain of unshakable faith. But when he heard Jezebel's threat, "he was afraid and arose and ran for his life and came to Beersheba, which belongs to Judah, and left his servant there" (19:3).

Beersheba was about a hundred miles south of Jezreel, but that still wasn't far enough away from wicked Jezebel. So Elijah went even farther into the wilderness; and there he sat, all alone, under a juniper tree.

And he prayed to die (v. 4).

An Interlude: Analysis of Disillusionment

As we look at this poor soul longing for death's relief, we ache with him. Why? Because we have visited that same juniper; and maybe we, too, have yearned for heaven's release. So for a few moments, let's examine five factors that led to his depression, factors that sometimes surface in our lives as well.

First: *Elijah was not thinking realistically or clearly.* When threatened by Jezebel, Elijah didn't consider the source—Jezebel was God's enemy, an idol worshiper, and had no authority over God's elect. Nor did Elijah question the threat itself. Could it have been just a bluff? And most importantly, Elijah neglected to immediately call upon the Lord. Like us in stressful situations, he forgot to stop and pray. Had he fallen on his knees before hightailing it south, he might have recaptured his sense of perspective in this situation.

Second: *Elijah had separated himself from relationships that strengthen.* Elijah kept his servant with him until Beersheba, but he went into the wilderness alone. Often, a discouraged person wants to escape from relationships. But depression feeds on loneliness, for we are most susceptible to its damaging effects when we are isolated from the strength friendships can bring (compare Eccles. 4:9–12).

Third: *Elijah was caught in the aftermath of a great victory.* Depression frequently comes on the heels of a great triumph. After all, everything in his life was built to serve this confrontation on Carmel. It's over. Now what does he do with the rest of his life? This extremely vulnerable time took him off guard, and he got caught in a Monday-morning quagmire. And fear gripped his heart.

Fourth: *Elijah was physically exhausted and emotionally spent.* During the last few years, Elijah's ministry had been full-speed ahead. And in the last few days, he had been riding the redline without any rest. When the adrenaline dried up, he was left physically and emotionally burned out. When that happens, our minds can play tricks on us, exaggerating every emotion into a vicious nightmare.

Fifth: *Elijah had submitted to the beast Self-pity.* "O Lord, take my life, for I am not better than my fathers" (1 Kings 19:4). But whoever said he had to be better than his fathers? His *self*-standard was perfection—this wasn't God's standard. But when he came up short, he felt sorry for himself. If he had let God set his goals, he would have been able to live within His measure; because God is always loving, always faithful, always accepting. Sometimes we just need to give ourselves a break.

At this point, some of us might be tempted to take Elijah by the shoulders and lovingly shake some sense into him. But the Lord has a different method.

The Response of the Lord

Instead of rebuking him, commanding him to get busy, loading guilt on him, or shaming his tender emotions, the Lord gently picks Elijah up and sets him on his feet again.

He Allowed Him Rest and Refreshment

The Lord knows that His man needs rest and nourishment; so, through a miraculous provision, God ministers to Elijah's physical needs.

> And he lay down and slept under a juniper tree; and behold, there was an angel touching him, and he said to him, "Arise, eat." Then he looked and behold, there was at his head a bread cake baked on hot stones, and a jar of water. So he ate and drank and lay down again. (vv. 5–6)

Like a loving nursemaid, the angel of the Lord tends to Elijah. It is beautiful to see how our God, who needs neither sleep nor nourishment, understands the physical needs of His people. God never expects us to be superhuman, so we should never feel negligent when we rest and play and laugh.

He Communicated Wisely with Elijah

Gently, tenderly, and with great insight, God speaks to Elijah: "Arise, eat, because the journey is too great for you" (v. 7b). Elijah responds by traveling forty days to Mount Horeb[2] in the strength of the food God had given him (v. 8). And there the Lord speaks to him again.

> Then he came there to a cave, and lodged there; and behold, the word of the Lord came to him, and He said to him, "What are you doing here, Elijah?" (v. 9)

Rather than issuing a command or rebuke, God simply asks him a question, which immediately opens the communication lines.

---

2. Mount Horeb is also known as Mount Sinai and has always been a significant meeting place for God and His people (compare Exod. 3, 19–20).

Elijah laments that he is all alone (v. 10); but instead of contradicting him,[3] God uses a different strategy.

> So He said, "Go forth, and stand on the mountain before the Lord." And behold, the Lord was passing by! And a great and strong wind was rending the mountains and breaking in pieces the rocks before the Lord; but the Lord was not in the wind. And after the wind an earthquake, but the Lord was not in the earthquake. And after the earthquake a fire, but the Lord was not in the fire; and after the fire a sound of a gentle blowing. And it came about when Elijah heard it, that he wrapped his face in his mantle, and went out and stood in the entrance of the cave. (vv. 11–13a)

God has no lecture for Elijah, only an object lesson. When we are depressed, feeling alone and unloved, God wants us to turn our eyes toward Him. And He comes to us in a "gentle blowing"—not in noise and commotion. So we should look for Him in the quietness of a starry sky or the stillness of a mountain meadow. Communion with God is best in our times of quiet.

But Elijah is still wrestling with his feelings. "And I alone am left; and they seek my life, to take it away" (v. 14b). Graciously, mercifully, God gives His prophet a glimpse of the future—a glimpse that reassures him that He still has a place and purpose for Elijah (vv. 15–17). Only after affirming Elijah's importance does God gently correct him—without criticism or impatience. "Yet I will leave 7,000 in Israel, all the knees that have not bowed to Baal and every mouth that has not kissed him" (v. 18).

He Gave Him a Close, Personal Friend

Foremost among those seven thousand is one man whom God chose to be Elijah's kindred spirit—Elisha. After saying good-bye to his parents, Elisha commits himself to the Lord's service. And the story concludes, "He arose and followed Elijah and ministered to him" (v. 21).

---

3. Even before confronting Ahab on Mount Carmel, Elijah knew that there were at least one hundred prophets still faithful to the Lord. They were hidden by Ahab's believing servant Obadiah (1 Kings 18:13).

This story ends happily with the two prophets shouldering the ministry together. Elijah has found his needed rest, companionship, and communion with the Lord.

A Final Thought

In John Bunyan's *The Pilgrim's Progress*, the main character, Christian, falls like Elijah into the Slough of Despond. Even with his cumbersome burden, Christian does not lose all hope; but he still cannot manage his way out of the mire. Finally, Help comes and assists him out of the pit. When Christian asks his new friend why this slough is here for travelers to stumble into, Help responds, "This miry slough is such a place as cannot be mended."[4]

Pits of despair that "cannot be mended" are likewise strewn throughout our lives. But the Lord is our Help, who with a firm but gentle hand can reach down and draw us out. And when our struggle is over we can turn back and thank the Giver of such unexpected gifts.

🍇 *Living Insights*

Al Capp had a terrific way of illustrating what it feels like to be depressed in the old cartoon strip *Li'l Abner*. Wherever the jinxed character Joe Btsfplk went, Al always drew a black rain cloud hanging just above his head. That is a perfect picture of depression— always gloomy, always dark, and always lonely. Everyone else seems to be romping in the sunshine, but for people like ol' Joe, the blues are ever present.

If God were drawing a cartoon of you right now, would He put a rain cloud above your head too? What kind would it be?

☐ A small cloud that comes and goes with the natural disappointments of life.

☐ A dreary, pervasive, foglike cloud that creeps into every nook and cranny.

☐ A crashing thunderhead that bears down on you, leaving you so fearful that you are unable to function.

4. John Bunyan, *The Pilgrim's Progress* (Old Tappan, N.J.: Fleming H. Revell Co., n.d.), p. 8.

Thankfully, God has designed us with the ability to process our feelings of loss and sadness, to grieve, and then to recover. This process works best when we have routinely shored up our foundation of emotional and physical well-being. Ask yourself the following questions, and pray for God's strength to build up the areas of your life that are vulnerable to out-of-control depression.

- When I experience a loss, on what should I focus my thoughts so that I can perceive the situation clearly?

  _____

  _____

- In what ways can my friendships be a strength to me when I'm discouraged?

  _____

  _____

- How can I refresh myself after an exhausting accomplishment in order to avoid depression?

  _____

  _____

- How do I rate my physical condition? What would help me become more physically energized?

  _____

  _____

- How have my thoughts about myself been affecting my attitude? In what ways can I be more positive and confident?

  _____

  _____

These five factors are vital in preventing depression. But what about the person who is already depressed? How can you be a support to that person? The answer to that question is the focus of Study Two.

Words of advice, such as "You should try reading your Bible" or "Think of all your blessings" or "God is disciplining you, and you need to confess your sin" are not a soothing balm to a person in depression. Those words can even force him or her into deeper guilt and frustration. Instead, we need to follow the Lord's example as He compassionately counseled Elijah.

First, He took care of Elijah's physical needs. Many times, severe depression is caused by a chemical imbalance in the body or other physical problems. If you have a friend in deep depression, that person may need to see a doctor. What doctors in your community understand depression and can offer advice? And how can you help provide your friend an opportunity for rest and refreshment?

_____

_____

_____

Also, the Lord communicated gently with Elijah. What can you do or say to that person to express your unconditional acceptance and love? Write down a few ideas.

_____

_____

_____

By giving him Elisha, the Lord also met Elijah's need for friend-ship. Listening attentively and relying on the Lord for wisdom will help you perceive your friend's real need. That need usually results from a loss in life, like the loss of respect or the loss of feeling loved. What loss do you think sparked your friend's depression? How can you help that person accept the loss?[5]

---

5. For further information on the subject of depression, we recommend *Happiness Is a Choice*, by Frank Minirth and Paul Meier; *Counseling the Depressed*, by Archibald Hart; and *Depression Hits Every Family*, by Grace Ketterman. Also, the Insight for Living Pastoral Ministries is available to answer any questions you may have. To contact one of the counselors, write to Insight for Living, Post Office Box 69000, Anaheim, CA 92817-0900.

Your friend's loss: _____

_____

How you can help your friend accept it: _____

_____

_____

_____

_____

    Ministering to the depressed is a long-term commitment. Are your resources becoming exhausted? The same God who refused to give up on Elijah offers the love and endurance you need today.

Chapter 8

WHEN GOD SAYS, "THAT'S ENOUGH!"

1 Kings 21:1–29

Rabbit had invited Fox to dinner—a first for these two. He had prepared a sumptuous meal and taken great pains to provide a pleasant atmosphere; and all things considered, Fox was intrigued.

Rabbit, an intellectual, said, "Fox, I invited you here tonight to discuss a concern of mine."

"Really?" asked Fox, with great interest.

"As I was saying, Fox, I think that every animal in the forest has the right to demand its own way. You know, get their just desserts."

Fox listened intently between bits of delicious delicacies; and while he did not find Rabbit's argument convincing, he was smart enough to visualize an interesting application of Rabbit's reasoning. He smacked his lips contemplatively.

Rabbit had just eaten his last lip-licking morsel and pulled his napkin from his neck, when Fox's eyes narrowed into thin lines. Rabbit, lulled by the comforts of good food and Fox's seeming congeniality, sat back in his chair with a contented sigh. All of a sudden, Fox sprang over the table and onto Rabbit . . . and ate him up for dessert.

Rabbit felt that his world would be improved if each animal could simply do as it pleased. If you subscribe to Rabbit's logic, don't be surprised when your philosophy eats you for dinner.[1] Two characters from Elijah's story found this out the hard way. But before we see their demise, let's take a broader look at the subject of divine judgment—the moment when God roars, "That's enough!"

General Revelation: Divine Judgment

It's a painful subject to address; but the truth of the matter is, there is a limit to God's patience. And if we're wise, we'll listen to what the Bible has to say about it. Here's just one example.

---

1. Based on John Warwick Montgomery, *The Law above the Law* (Minneapolis, Minn.: Bethany Fellowship, Dimension Books, 1975), pp. 17–18.

A man who hardens his neck after much reproof
Will suddenly be broken beyond remedy.
(Prov. 29:1)

A stiff-necked person is one who hears correction but stubbornly refuses to respond. An easy attitude to take, but one with dire consequences. The words at the end of this proverb, "beyond remedy," are rarely used in Scripture; usually, we see God cradling us within His compassion and showering us with mercy and grace. But when someone continually and deliberately makes rebellious choices, God intervenes, first by trying to get that person's attention, but then, faced with a willfully turned back, with destruction that is immediate and final (see also Prov. 6:12–15).

The Bible records at least three examples of God saying, "That's enough!" First, unable to find even ten righteous men between them, God visited His wrath on the twin cities of Sodom and Gomorrah, raining fire and brimstone on them until nothing was left, not even a blade of grass (19:24–25).

The second scene involves Herod Agrippa, who reveled in glory meant only for God . . . and paid with his life. He allowed the people to cry out that he was a god, not a man; but God proved Herod's mortality with the most earthly of deaths—he was eaten by worms (Acts 12:21–23).

Our last tragic picture concerns the northern kingdom of Israel, for here an entire nation fell under the well-earned wrath of God. Not only did King Zedekiah harden his heart against the Lord, but even the priests and the people were unfaithful, going so far as to defile the house of the Lord in Jerusalem. God sent warnings to them again and again, but His messengers were only mocked, until finally "the wrath of the Lord arose against His people, until there was no remedy" (2 Chron. 36:16; see also vv. 11–15).

As if these three weren't enough, another echo of God's heart-shattering "That's enough!" resounds through Elijah's story as well, though it was prompted not by him, but by—who else—Ahab and Jezebel. And what happens to them, though certainly deserved, stands as a frightful reminder to us today.

Specific Illustration: Ahab and Jezebel

Unrestrained desire respects self—only. Others get savagely plowed under in its path, as does an unobtrusive and law-observing farmer named Naboth when Ahab desires his vineyard.

66

The Vineyard

Ahab, the king, has his eye on a nice tract of land next to his palace in Samaria. But it is owned by Naboth, a simple man from Jezreel. So Ahab, approaching him as a potential buyer, sets the terms in a congenial way—"Whatever you want, Naboth, I'll make it work, in land or money" (1 Kings 21:2). What he had not counted on was Naboth's reply.

> "The Lord forbid me that I should give you the inheritance of my fathers." (v. 3)

Naboth had no problem with Ahab personally, but he felt an obligation to the Lord's Word about his own family property (see Lev. 25:23; Num. 36:7). The story should have ended here, but tragically, it doesn't. Naboth's unexpected response casts a dark cloud over Ahab's formerly sunny day.

> So Ahab came into his house sullen and vexed because of the word which Naboth the Jezreelite had spoken to him. . . . And he lay down on his bed and turned away his face and ate no food. (v. 4)

Like a small boy who fails to get his way, he picks up his marbles and goes home, pouting all the way. Once there, he throws himself down on his bed and refuses to eat, which soon captures his wife's attention. Jezebel, as she hears her husband's pitiful story, feels personally affronted. And regrettably, her domineering spirit rises.

> And Jezebel his wife said to him, "Do you now reign over Israel? Arise, eat bread, and let your heart be joyful; I will give you the vineyard of Naboth the Jezreelite." (v. 7)

Seizing the moment, she concocts a witch's brew of bubbling curses to spew upon unsuspecting Naboth, all in the name of the king.

> So she wrote letters in Ahab's name and sealed them with his seal, and sent letters to the elders and to the nobles who were living with Naboth in his city. Now she wrote in the letters, saying, "Proclaim a fast, and seat Naboth at the head of the people; and seat two worthless men before him, and let them testify against him, saying, 'You cursed God and the

king.' Then take him out and stone him to death."[2]
(vv. 8–10)

Her strategy works. But little does she realize that the poison she's pouring over Naboth will spill over into her own life.

The Murder

In response to what they presumed to be the king's letter, the corrupt leaders of Jezreel convene a public fast (vv. 11–13a). Naboth is summoned, and sitting across from him are two despicable characters whose sole purpose is to defame him. Under the guise of justice, they stand at the right time, point their fingers, and say, "Naboth cursed God and the king" (v. 13b). A gasp rises from the crowd, and immediately the magistrate orders his execution.[3]

> So they took him outside the city and stoned him to death with stones. (v. 13c)

Cold-blooded, premeditated murder—all to satiate the unbridled desire of the royal couple.

The Response

> Then they sent word to Jezebel, saying, "Naboth has been stoned, and is dead." And . . . Jezebel said to Ahab, "Arise, take possession of the vineyard of Naboth, the Jezreelite, which he refused to give you for money; for Naboth is not alive, but dead." (vv. 14–15)

While Ahab and Jezebel do a few high fives, another response is taking place in heaven. God Himself has been tracking this fiasco

---

2. "Jezebel ordered the fasting for a sign, as though some public crime or heavy load of guilt rested upon the city, for which it was necessary that it should humble itself before God. . . . The intention was, that at the very outset the appearance of justice should be given to the legal process about to be instituted in the eyes of all the citizens, and the stamp of veracity impressed upon the crime of which Naboth was to be accused. . . . God and king are mentioned together . . . to put him to death as a blasphemer of God, according to Deut. 13:11 and 17:5. . . . Blaspheming the king is not to be taken as a second crime to be added to the blasphemy of God; but blaspheming the king, as the visible representative of God, was *co ipso* also blaspheming God." C. F. Keil and F. Delitzsch, *Commentary on the Old Testament*, trans. James Martin (reprint, Grand Rapids, Mich.: William B. Eerdmans Publishing Co., 1978), vol. 3, pp. 270–71.

3. Second Kings 9:26 reveals that Naboth's sons, too, were put to death to give the king clear access to the property.

and has had it up to here. And who does He send to tell Ahab? You guessed it—Elijah.

> "Arise, go down to meet Ahab king of Israel, who is in Samaria; behold, he is in the vineyard of Naboth where he has gone down to take possession of it. And you shall speak to him, saying, 'Thus says the Lord, "Have you murdered, and also taken possession?"' And you shall speak to him, saying, 'Thus says the Lord, "In the place where the dogs licked up the blood of Naboth the dogs shall lick up your blood, even yours."'" (vv. 18–19)

The Prediction

Elijah finds Ahab where the Lord said he would be, in Naboth's fields, relishing the thought of fall vegetables. Imagine the king's face when he turns to see Elijah. "Have you found me, O my enemy?" he cries (v. 20a). And Elijah responds with the passion of one on a mission from God.

> "I have found you, because you have sold yourself to do evil in the sight of the Lord. Behold, I will bring evil upon you, and will utterly sweep you away, and will cut off from Ahab every male, both bond and free in Israel; and I will make your house like the house of Jeroboam . . . because of the provocation with which you have provoked Me to anger, and because you have made Israel sin. And of Jezebel also has the Lord spoken, saying, 'The dogs shall eat Jezebel in the district of Jezreel.' The one belonging to Ahab, who dies in the city, the dogs shall eat, and the one who dies in the field the birds of heaven shall eat." (vv. 20b–24)

Ahab must have been shaking in his sandals. Like it or not, he knew by now that if Elijah said it, it would happen. And later on it does . . . word for word.

> And the battle raged that day, and the king was propped up in his chariot in front of the Arameans, and died at evening, and the blood from the wound ran into the bottom of the chariot. . . . And they washed the chariot by the pool of Samaria, and the

dogs licked up the blood (now the harlots bathed themselves there), according to the word of the Lord which He spoke. (22:35, 38)

In unmistakable terms, God had said, "That's enough!"

Personal Appropriation: Today

How God dealt with Ahab, and how He deals with us as well, can be boiled down to three principles.

There is an end to God's patience, and no one knows when it will come. An end will come for all who reject God's warnings . . . in His time and in His way. How much better to respond as Elijah did with each God-given assignment than to hear God's voice of warning as Ahab did . . . and ignore it time and again. This truth serves as a serious warning to anyone who stubbornly refuses to acknowledge God's voice.

God keeps His promise, and no one stops it. Though God gave Ahab and Jezebel opportunity after opportunity to repent, they abused His mercy and patience and took it to mean that they could endlessly get away with anything. Solomon summarized this line of thinking when he wrote:

> Because the sentence against an evil deed is not executed quickly, therefore the hearts of the sons of men among them are given fully to do evil. (Eccles. 8:11)

However, God is not slack in dealing with evil, and He will not allow His patience to be abused. He *will* perform what He promises, and no one can stop it.

God acknowledges humility, and no one should refuse it. You can't get any more evil than Ahab (1 Kings 21:25–26); humanly speaking, there should have been no hope for him. But because at one point Ahab "tore his clothes and put on sackcloth and fasted" before the Lord (v. 27), God responded with mercy.

> "Do you see how Ahab has humbled himself before Me? Because he has humbled himself before Me, I will not bring the evil in his days, but I will bring the evil upon his house in his son's days." (v. 29)

Unfortunately, Ahab's humble attitude was short-lived, and his tendency to invoke God's wrath continued. But we can find hope in God's generous response to Ahab's momentary humility: Although evil reduces your stature before God, you are never as tall as when you humbly reach for His mercy, acknowledging and confessing your wrongs to Him.

Living Insights

Ahab and Jezebel had always lived as they pleased, as though there were no such thing as offending God. Then Elijah arrived and injected a heavy dose of God's truth into their lives. And they didn't like it.

If an Elijah were to step into your life, what do you think God would have him say?

_____

_____

What would your response be? Would you feel angry? Threatened? Humbled? Honestly examine your heart.

_____

_____

Though repeatedly confronted with the reality of God and the truth of His word, Ahab and Jezebel continued to "harden their necks" and abuse God's patience. Has God been tapping you on the shoulder lately? If you are resisting His promptings, what do you think the consequences will be?

In one year? _____

_____

In five years? _____

_____

How do you think it will affect those you love?

_____

_____

_____

If you are resisting God, what do you think is at the root of this attitude?

_____

_____

Sometimes comparison can keep us from dealing with our own issues. We can say to ourselves, "I'm not as bad as so-and-so down the street" or "It's not like I'm a child molester or something" or "I've never done anything as bad as Ahab and Jezebel!" But when you compare yourself with another person, you are only distracting yourself from the truth God has circled in your own life.

Another method of resistance, perhaps the devil's sharpest tool, is procrastination. This only gives your neck a chance to grow stiffer and your ears to become duller, rather than actually helping stop the problem.

If you are leaning toward persistent sin, please stop resisting God's proddings and reconsider Ahab and Jezebel's story. And follow Ahab's humble course of action . . . before God says, "That's enough!" to you.

🍇 *Living Insights*   STUDY TWO

While God's patience has a long fuse, anyone who fails to turn away from evil eventually ignites an all-consuming fire. Even after Ahab's death, Jezebel and her sons kept holding a flame to that fuse until the wick was gone; and God struck His own match, inflaming an unquenchable fire that would fulfill His promise of destruction to Ahab's family. Read the story for yourself in 2 Kings 9:1–37; 10:1–11 before continuing.

Fulfillment of God's Word

The first tragedy occurs in 9:23–24. What is it? _____

_____

The next tragedy is recorded in verses 30–37. Who dies? _____

_____

How? _____

What impresses you most about this scene? _____

_____

_____

_____

After this, another tragedy quickly follows in 10:1–11. Who dies?

_____

Why? _____

What impresses you most here? _____

_____

Finally, the last tragedy comes in verses 9–11. Who dies? _____

Why? _____

What do you learn from this? _____

_____

Response

> Do not be deceived, God is not mocked; for what-
> ever a man sows, this he will also reap. (Gal. 6:7)

What are you sowing in your life? If it isn't something you'd like to reap, then stop now and turn your heart to God. Build up and nourish those around you. By doing so, you guarantee that God will never say to you, "That's enough!"

Chapter 9

SATANIC FLIES THAT SWARM AROUND US

1 Kings 22:51–53; 2 Kings 1:1–18

James A. Pike, a noted and controversial lawyer-turned-cleric-turned-church-dropout, was devastated when his oldest son committed suicide. Shortly after this tragic event, he began experiencing a series of psychic events which eventually led to a major change in his beliefs.

Previously denying any existence after death, Pike came to believe that the spirit of his son had lived on. He began consulting one of England's most celebrated mediums, Ena Twigg, who urged him to contact an organization in the United States that would give him access to other mediums.

Each medium he used gave predictions that the future proved true. He became hooked, absorbed with the subject of life after death. He increasingly sought contact with the other side; and unfortunately, millions of people followed his search and also entered a dangerous and forbidden realm of darkness. Pike's obsessive search ended with his mysterious death in 1969 in Israel, in the arid desert near the Dead Sea.[1]

Ironically, centuries earlier in Israel—less than a hundred miles away from the scene of James Pike's death—a king's son, Ahaziah, also sought a forbidden source of comfort. And it cost him his life too.

Historical Setting: The Reign of Ahaziah

Ahaziah comes on the scene after his infamous father, Ahab, dies in battle (1 Kings 22:37–38, 40). The crown is passed to him—one more in the line of Israel's evil kings; for although a change of rulers may have taken place, Ahaziah doesn't stray from the dark religious convictions of his parents.

---

1. Merrill F. Unger, *The Mystery of Bishop Pike* (Wheaton, Ill.: Tyndale House Publishers, 1971).

Ahaziah the son of Ahab became king over Israel in Samaria in the seventeenth year of Jehoshaphat king of Judah, and he reigned two years over Israel. And he did evil in the sight of the Lord and walked in the way of his father and in the way of his mother and in the way of Jeroboam the son of Nebat, who caused Israel to sin. So he served Baal and worshiped him and provoked the Lord God of Israel to anger according to all that his father had done. (vv. 51–53)

Ahaziah's Fall, Disastrous Decision

You'd think Ahaziah would have learned from his father's mistakes, but instead he follows in his footsteps. A tragic event in his home sets the stage for Ahaziah to consult the dark side.

And Ahaziah fell through the lattice in his upper chamber which was in Samaria, and became ill. (2 Kings 1:2a)

Bedridden from his fall, Ahaziah worries that he might not ever recover. So he decides to take matters into his own hands and see exactly what the future holds.

So he sent messengers and said to them, "Go, inquire of Baal-zebub, the god of Ekron, whether I shall recover from this sickness." (v. 2b)

Little does he realize that, by seeking out the deadly enemies of God, he has just signed his own death warrant.

God of Ekron: *Baal-zebub*

Just who is this "Baal-zebub" Ahaziah seeks? A linguistic look at the name will give us a clue. Two Hebrew words combine to form this god's name: *Baal,* meaning "lord or god," and *zebub*, a noun meaning "fly." Therefore, Baal-zebub literally means "god of the flies." Scholars are not certain whether this was a god who at Ekron protected people from diseases caused by flies or whether it was an idol in the form of a fly. But whatever the exact meaning, one thing is sure: Baal-zebub's followers offered predictions of the future. That's why Ahaziah sought their services.

We get further insight into the nature of this Fly-god by following his flight pattern into the New Testament. Eight centuries later his activities showed up in Jesus' time.[2] We can read of him in the story of Jesus healing the blind and dumb man who was also demon-possessed (Matt. 12:22–23). Afterward, the people wondered if this Nazareth-raised, Bethlehem-born carpenter's son—Jesus—could be Messiah. The shifting crowd, straining to see both Jesus and the healed man, included religious professionals who felt that the crowd's idea needed to be challenged.

> But when the Pharisees heard it, they said, "This man casts out demons only by Beelzebul the ruler of the demons." (v. 24)

Notice how they described Beelzebul: "the ruler of the demons." There is no doubt that the Fly-god, Baal-zebub, was also empowered by the demonic world.[3] But Jesus' deliverance of the blind and dumb man reveals that His power is greater than that of any demon.

Encounters with Elijah

Lying impatiently in bed, Ahaziah sends messengers to inquire of Ekron's satanic god. However, they run into a problem: Elijah.

God's Message

Not wanting His people anywhere near Ekron, God has sent Elijah to intercept the royal mission.

> But the angel of the Lord said to Elijah the Tishbite, "Arise, go up to meet the messengers of the king of Samaria and say to them, 'Is it because there is no God in Israel that you are going to inquire of Baal-zebub, the god of Ekron?' Now therefore thus says the Lord, 'You shall not come down from the bed where you have gone up, but you shall surely die.'" Then Elijah departed. (2 Kings 1:3–4)

Ahaziah's Messengers

When the couriers are confronted by God's prophet and His message, they immediately abort their quest and return to the palace,

---

2. The name Baal-zebub appears in the Old Testament four times, all in the first chapter of 2 Kings (vv. 2, 3, 6, 16). The Greek equivalent, Beelzebul, appears seven times in the gospels of the New Testament (Matt. 10:25; 12:24, 27; Mark 3:22; Luke 11:15, 18, 19).

3. In 1 Corinthians 10:19–20, we are told that idols are nothing in themselves; but they represent a working ground for demonic powers.

where the king lies waiting for their word. "Back so soon?" the king asks, and his men quickly tell him why (vv. 5–6). Ahaziah, with a sneaking suspicion, prods them for more information.

> And he said to them, "What kind of man was he who came up to meet you and spoke these words to you?" (v. 7)

And these diplomatic couriers fill in the blanks for their sovereign.

> "He was a hairy man with a leather girdle bound about his loins." And [Ahaziah] said, "It is Elijah the Tishbite." (v. 8)

A growl of recognition marks the king's voice. His family has had problems with this man before; he is always countering their innovative programs. And now this. Ahaziah decides it's time to fight back.

> Then the king sent to him a captain of fifty with his fifty. And he went up to him, and behold, he was sitting on the top of the hill. And he said to him, "O man of God, the king says, 'Come down.'" And Elijah answered and said to the captain of fifty, "If I am a man of God, let fire come down from heaven and consume you and your fifty." Then fire came down from heaven and consumed him and his fifty. (vv. 9–10)

Undaunted, Ahaziah sends a second company—and the same thing happens (vv. 11–12). By now the captains at home are getting nervous. They may be next! Sure enough, His Highness sends a third company of men to overwhelm Elijah. But this time a wise captain humbles himself before the prophet.

> He came and bowed down on his knees before Elijah, and begged him and said to him, "O man of God, please let my life and the lives of these fifty servants of yours be precious in your sight. Behold fire came down from heaven, and consumed the first two captains of fifty with their fifties; but now let my life be precious in your sight." And the angel of the Lord said to Elijah, "Go down with him; do not be afraid of him." So he arose and went down with him to the king. (vv. 13–15)

Whew. The captain relaxes. And everyone, including Elijah, walks to Samaria to see the king.

What must Ahaziah think as this fiery prophet approaches him? This is their first meeting, and it will be their last.

Elijah's Message

> Then [Elijah] said to him, "Thus says the Lord, 'Because you have sent messengers to inquire of Baal-zebub, the god of Ekron—is it because there is no God in Israel to inquire of His word?—therefore you shall not come down from the bed where you have gone up, but shall surely die.'" (v. 16)

Fatal words. "Listen, Ahaziah, you have substituted the true for the false. You have turned to the world's solutions and rejected the Lord." And swiftly the consequences follow.

> So Ahaziah died according to the word of the Lord which Elijah had spoken. And because he had no son, Jehoram became king in his place in the second year of Jehoram the son of Jehoshaphat, king of Judah. (vv. 17–18)

Truth for Today

Many people seek information about the future through present-day Baal-zebubs, such as mediums, astrology, palmistry, and Satanism. These, plus newspapers, magazines, computer software, and films are pandering the ways of darkness. May the three lessons we learned from Ahaziah's life indelibly impact your resolve to never dabble in the occult.

First: *God is displeased with any occult involvement.* Scripture gives ample warning: The occult, whether in the form of white or black magic, spiritism, seances, or any other expressions of darkness[4] are off-limits to a person following the Lord.

> "'Do not turn to mediums or spiritists; do not seek them out to be defiled by them. I am the Lord your God.'" (Lev. 19:31)

4. Two good resources on this topic are Merrill F. Unger's *Demons in the World Today* (Wheaton, Ill.: Tyndale House Publishers, 1971), and *Biblical Demonology*, 6th ed. (Wheaton, Ill.: Scripture Press, 1965). The latter work gives an excellent explanation of Saul's encounter with the medium of Endor (see pp. 148–52).

"'As for the person who turns to mediums and to spiritists, to play the harlot after them, I will also set My face against that person and will cut him off from among his people.'" (20:6)[5]

These are loving statements from One who knows these things better than we ever could. Occult activities carry a high price tag—they are easy to embrace, but not so easily released.

Second: *God is dishonored by pursuits of the future apart from His Word.* The future draws people to satisfy their curiosity; when opportunities arise to peer into the future, they are difficult to resist. But when we look to sources like astrology and card laying, it is like a slap in the face of God, who asks us to trust only Him for our future.

So the next time knowledge of the future presents itself under the guise of any form but the Bible, turn your heart to the Lord and resist the magnetic pull. He is pleased when you do.

Third: *God is delighted when we turn to His Word and trust Him only.* This may seem far less exciting than contacting the spirit world; but when you turn to the Lord, you honor His evaluation of a whole sphere of illegitimate activity. Your rejection of any occult involvement acknowledges that He knows best; and you wisely steer clear of the swarming flies of satanic turmoil and disruption.

Living Insights

STUDY ONE

Are you aware of how specific God's commands are concerning occult involvement?

> "When you enter the land which the Lord your God gives you, you shall not learn to imitate the detestable things of those nations. There shall not be found among you anyone who makes his son or his daughter pass through the fire, one who uses divination, one who practices witchcraft, or one who interprets omens, or a sorcerer, or one who casts a spell, or a medium, or a spiritist, or one who calls up the dead. For whoever does these things is detestable to the Lord; and because of these detestable

5. Other key references to the occult are Deuteronomy 18:9–12; Isaiah 47:11–15; Jeremiah 10:1–5.

things the Lord your God will drive them out before you. You shall be blameless before the Lord your God." (Deut. 18:9–13)

Many people—Christians included—get involved in occult activities thinking that they're fun and harmless things to do. But harmless, powerless, they are not. And to remain unaware of that truth is to leave yourself frighteningly unprotected against Satan's deadly games.

Have you allowed the occult to make even the smallest inroad into your life? Perhaps you've never sought out a medium, but do you read your horoscope—just for kicks? Do you visit the fortune-teller at the county fair? Do you bring out the Ouija board or tarot cards to spice up a party? Write down, bring into the light, any areas of darkness you are playing with.

_____

_____

Has your involvement affected you or others? How?

_____

_____

Do you fully realize who is behind these activities? Read John 8:44, 1 Peter 5:8, and Revelation 12:10, and write down his true identity.

_____

_____

Do you really think he just wants you to have a little harmless fun? He who prowls about like a roaring lion seeking whom he may devour most certainly has more in store for you than that. So don't leave yourself open and vulnerable to this deceitful enemy. He may appear as an angel of light (2 Cor. 11:14), but in him is immeasurable darkness.

With this in mind, then, commit yourself to staying away from *any* involvement with the occult. Throw away your Ouija board, tarot cards, and all other paraphernalia. Stop reading your horoscope. Do whatever you have to, to close the door on this area.

Don't play with demons, because they will not play by your rules.

Perhaps dabbling in the occult has never been an issue for you. You've always understood its dark nature and have therefore always known to stay away from it. But what about your children?

Out of the protective eye of their parents, children can innocently be drawn into this realm through simple games and experimentation with their playmates. Their curious, exploring minds are wonderful gifts—but they need loving guidance to keep them out of harm's way.

Have you ever talked about the occult and God's commands concerning it with your children? If not, use this time to outline what you would say.

_____

_____

_____

_____

_____

If, in your talk with your children, you discover that they have experimented with the occult, try to stay calm and respond in a caring, balanced way. They don't need to be shamed for being curious; they need to be protected from Satan gaining a foothold in their minds.

God wants the best for your children—and they need to know that this is what's ultimately behind His "no" to the occult. To help this truth become a part of your children's hearts, set aside some time this week to memorize this verse with them:

> " 'For I know the plans that I have for you,' declares
> the Lord, 'plans for welfare and not for calamity to
> give you a future and a hope.' " (Jer. 29:11)

God offers a future with a hope . . . something Satan would never do.

Chapter 10

A NO-DEATH CONTRACT
2 Kings 2:1–14

Ultimately, an end comes to everything. But the "end" that awaits Elijah is hardly an ending; it's more like a glorious beginning, a passage through eternity's open portal. For the fiery prophet doesn't age gracefully and then quietly die—he doesn't die at all!

As we approach the prophet's end, God will "take up Elijah by a whirlwind to heaven" (2 Kings 2:1)—in one deathless stride he will step from the temporal into the everlasting. And God has told him that today's the day.

What would you do if you knew today was your last day on earth? Perhaps you, like Elijah, would revisit those places in your heart that have meant the most to you.

Reflection: Places of Meaning

As heaven's light begins to dawn in Elijah's life, he thinks through the glimpses of eternity that have shaped him.

Gilgal, Place of Beginnings

> And it came about when the Lord was about to take up Elijah by a whirlwind to heaven, that Elijah went with Elisha from Gilgal. (2 Kings 2:1)

His journey to heaven begins at Gilgal, a place of historic beginnings for Israel. It was here that the infant nation took its first steps into the Promised Land (Josh. 4:19–24). It was their beachhead, their place of security and safety.

We, too, have our Gilgals—the places of our beginnings in the life of Christ. Here we were nurtured by our Father's love and became secure in Him. Here we gained strength by getting into the Word of God, by learning to pray, by seeking to be alone with the Lord. And it is from this start, this Gilgal, that we go like Elijah to Bethel.

Bethel, Place of Altar

> And Elijah said to Elisha, "Stay here please, for the Lord has sent me as far as Bethel." But Elisha said,

> "As the Lord lives and as you yourself live, I will not
> leave you." So they went down to Bethel. Then the
> sons of the prophets[1] who were at Bethel came out
> to Elisha and said to him, "Do you know that the
> Lord will take away your master from over you today?"
> And he said, "Yes, I know; be still." (vv. 2–3)

Sticking close to his master's side, Elisha is determined to walk
all fifteen miles from Gilgal to Bethel with Elijah. When they arrive,
they are met by Israel's seminarians, who remind Elisha of the sig-
nificance of this day. But Elisha wants to protect Elijah's desire for
quiet reflection, and he responds, "Shhhhh. Let him have these
moments to himself."

So Elijah is able to walk undistracted through Bethel,[2] contem-
plating this place where Abraham and Jacob had erected altars to
the Lord (Gen. 12:8; 28:10–19). Surely Elijah's thoughts wandered
to his own altars: the brook Cherith, the widow's kitchen table,
the spare room where her boy came back to life. Painful places, but
places of great meaning.

Our Bethels also speak of sacrifice and hurt. They are places
where we are forced to surrender to God things precious to us: a
loved one, unrealized dreams, a loss of a job or relationship. Add
sickness, helplessness, and the world's demands to the list, and you
understand Bethel even more. It is our altar where we resolve our
need to fully trust the Lord.

From the bittersweet memories of Bethel, Elijah next seeks to
face Jericho.

Jericho, Place of Battle

> And Elijah said to him, "Elisha, please stay here,
> for the Lord has sent me to Jericho." But he said,
> "As the Lord lives, and as you yourself live, I will
> not leave you." So they came to Jericho. And the
> sons of the prophets who were at Jericho approached
> Elisha and said to him, "Do you know that the Lord
> will take away your master from over you today?"
> And he answered, "Yes, I know; be still." (vv. 4–5)

---

1. *"Gilgal* and *Bethel* . . . were seats of schools of the prophets, which Elijah had founded
in the kingdom of the ten tribes." C. F. Keil and F. Delitzsch, *Commentary on the Old
Testament,* trans. James Martin (reprint, Grand Rapids, Mich.: William B. Eerdmans Publishing Co., 1978), vol. 3, p. 290.

2. Bethel means "house of God."

Once again, Elijah leaves the door open for Elisha to make a comfortable exit, but the apprentice prophet remains faithful. So twelve miles later, the pair reaches Jericho; and Elisha sensitively hushes a second group of prophets for his master's sake.

What will Elijah recall in Jericho? Joshua's bold leadership, the clarion blast of rams' horns, the walls of that once mighty fortress in ruins. He may also retrace his own battles: with Ahab and his sinister wife Jezebel, with the frenzied prophets of useless stone gods, with Ahaziah and his arrogant messengers. In retrospect, Elijah sees how his life has been used to cause the collapse of Israel's spiritual apostasy—a resounding victory no less significant than Joshua's.

What have your Jerichos been? Perhaps you waged a battle of survival in your teen years. Maybe you have wrestled with emotional or spiritual issues. Whatever your battleground, you have learned, like Elijah, that without the Lord's help all is lost.

After one last look, Elijah turns to his final earthly destination: the River Jordan.

The Jordan, Place of Death

Still determined to allow Elisha a choice, Elijah says again,

> "Please stay here, for the Lord has sent me to the Jordan." And he said, "As the Lord lives, and as you yourself live, I will not leave you." So the two of them went on.
> Now fifty men of the sons of the prophets went and stood opposite them at a distance, while the two of them stood by the Jordan. (vv. 6–7)

Even the "sons of the prophets" know this will be Elijah's last river crossing; so, silently and expectantly, they watch the two men of God approach the Jordan.

Reaching the threshold of his farewell, Elijah lingers over shadows of death that have passed over his life. He remembers his flight into the Negev, where he asked the Lord to let him die (1 Kings 19:4b). Helpless in depression's grip, all hope for life was completely squeezed from him (v. 10). But now, at the Jordan, he shakes his head and marvels at how his life was spared—and how he had to die to selfishness to live for the Lord.

Our Jordans are like that too. Only we will face a Jordan Elijah never did—physical death. Some of us have come to that river's edge and are about to cross over. Others, perhaps most, have a child or a loved one who has journeyed on before. And spiritually, we have all been wrenched, pulled, and twisted by our jobs, families, personal circumstances. These things have shaped us, hopefully making us kinder, more generous, and more sensitive to the Lord. This is our spiritual passage across the River Jordan.

Now only one small step is left for Elijah. Jordan's placid and lazy water flows past him, tiny eddies swirling here and there, completely unaffected by his thoughts . . . until he removes his outer cloak and slaps the water.

Separation: Words of Departure

> And Elijah took his mantle and folded it together and struck the waters, and they were divided here and there, so that the two of them crossed over on dry ground. (2 Kings 2:8)

Can't you just hear the fifty prophets marvel as they raise up on their toes, straining for a better view? "Wow, did you see that?" Praises, too, no doubt fell from their lips.

Once on the other side of the river, Elijah desires to reward his faithful friend.

> Now it came about when they had crossed over, that Elijah said to Elisha, "Ask what I shall do for you before I am taken from you." And Elisha said, "Please, let a double portion of your spirit be upon me." (v. 9)

Fully aware of God's need to continue the work Elijah has started, Elisha recognizes his part of the Lord's plan. His vision of how God can use him is unlimited. So Elijah thoughtfully processes his friend's request.

> And he said, "You have asked a hard thing. Nevertheless, if you see me when I am taken from you, it shall be so for you; but if not, it shall not be so." (v. 10)

Since Elisha's spirit has tenaciously clung to Elijah all along their journey, is there any doubt that Elisha would never leave his friend's sight?

> Then it came about as they were going along and talking, that behold, there appeared a chariot of fire and horses of fire which separated the two of them.

> And Elijah went up by a whirlwind to heaven. And
> Elisha saw it and cried out, "My father, my father,
> the chariots of Israel and its horsemen!" And he saw
> him no more. (vv. 11–12a)

Elijah's journey to heaven is just as God had described it earlier
(v. 1). And Elisha does see the astonishing flurry of God's chariot
and the whirlwind whisking Elijah up and away until he disappears
in the blue above.

Continuation: Mantle of Power

> Then [Elisha] took hold of his own clothes and tore
> them in two pieces. He also took up the mantle of
> Elijah that fell from him, and returned and stood
> by the bank of the Jordan. And he took the mantle
> of Elijah that fell from him, and struck the waters
> and said, "Where is the Lord, the God of Elijah?"
> And when he also had struck the waters, they were
> divided here and there; and Elisha crossed over.
> (vv. 12b–14)

Elisha has just lost his dearest friend. But while Elijah's life has
ended, Elisha's life of ministry is just beginning. From Elisha's response of pressing on in the face of grief, we can glean two wonderful
principles.

First: *When a person of God dies, nothing of God dies.* Though
Elijah has been taken from among the prophets, God still remains
actively interested in His people's welfare. He will provide leaders
to look after and guide His loved ones.

Second: *When the work of a great person is finished, the beginning
of another is started.* With Elijah's earthly wick snuffed out, Elisha's
light emerges with God's blessing and power.

🍇 *Living Insights* STUDY ONE

Just as Elijah paused to review his life, so we need time to reflect
on ours. Linger awhile at each of the places where Elijah stopped,
and put some of your memories on paper. In doing so, you will have
taken the first steps in creating a journal that will safeguard trea-
sured lessons you've learned on the sacred journey of life.

Gilgal—home base. This place marks the roots of your Christian experience. Recall the key elements—people, places, events—that led to your faith and early growth in Christ.

_____

_____

_____

_____

Bethel—place of surrender. This is a painful place to experience, especially when you are forced to surrender to God things dear to your heart. Have you spent time here? What have your experiences at the altar been like?

_____

_____

_____

_____

Jericho—place of attack. Jericho means battles. It is a place where every conceivable onslaught comes up against you: your own rights versus others' and God's; your struggles both emotionally and spiritually; a myriad of disappointments, depression, and frustration, even disillusionment. Describe the greatest battle you've ever faced and how you handled it.

_____

_____

_____

_____

Jordan River—place of death. The Jordan can represent our spiritual death to selfishness and our old sin nature. Have you crossed this river spiritually? What brought you to its banks, and what were you like when you emerged?

_____

_____

The Jordan can also signify life's end physically. If you are facing the river's edge, what kind of impact has this had on your life and values?

_____

_____

_____

_____

What would you like to leave behind for others?

_____

_____

_____

_____

Just as He did for Elijah, God will take us through our Gilgals, Bethels, Jerichos, and Jordans. *And beyond.* For we, too—if our faith rests in Christ—will someday be ushered into heaven's home . . . into Immanuel's land.

> The sands of time are sinking,
>   The dawn of heaven breaks;
> The summer morn I've sighed for—
>   The fair, sweet morn awakes:
> Dark, dark hath been the midnight,
>   But dayspring is at hand,
> And glory, glory dwelleth
>   In Immanuel's land.[3]

3. Anne Ross Cousin, "The Sands of Time Are Sinking."

> Elijah was not only a spokesperson of the word; he
> was himself a living word, proclaiming through his
> name and life-style his wholehearted and exclusive
> devotion to God.[4]

What have the words of Elijah's life spoken to you? In the space
provided, write down the flashes of insight and truth that mean the
most to you from our study of this fiery prophet.

Standing Alone in the Gap _____

_____

Boot Camp at Cherith _____

_____

Advanced Training at Zarephath _____

_____

A Miracle in the Home _____

_____

The God Who Answers by Fire _____

_____

Kneeling on the Promises _____

_____

Sure Cure for the Blues _____

_____

When God Says, "That's Enough!" _____

_____

4. Gene Rice, *Nations under God: A Commentary on the Book of 1 Kings* (Grand Rapids,
Mich.: William B. Eerdmans Publishing Co., 1990), p. 145.

Satanic Flies That Swarm Around Us _____

_____

A No-Death Contract _____

_____

———◆———

BOOKS FOR
PROBING FURTHER

God used one man, Elijah, to bring an entire nation back to Himself—a people nearly swallowed up in darkness by Jezebel's treacherous idolatry. And because this one man had "a nature like ours" (James 5:17), we are given hope that we, too, can pierce the darkness of our times with the light of God's truth. The following books explore some of the issues we have in common with Elijah and are presented to encourage you to shine brightly where your influence is observed and felt.

His Stand against His Times

Schlossberg, Herbert. *Idols for Destruction: Christian Faith and Its Confrontation with American Society.* Nashville, Tenn.: Thomas Nelson Publishers, 1983. Addressing the great despair in our society head-on, Schlossberg—in a scholarly treatment—uncovers the biblical reasons for it and helps us know how to stand in the gap against it.

His Isolation at Cherith

Elliot, Elisabeth. *Loneliness.* Nashville, Tenn.: Thomas Nelson Publishers, Oliver Nelson, 1988. Loneliness touches each of us at some point in our lives. This excellent treatment of the subject will give you alternatives to your isolation, helping you to turn your wilderness into a pathway to God.

His Move to Zarephath

Rinehart, Paula. *Whatever Happened to the Sunday School Class of '66.* Nashville, Tenn.: Thomas Nelson Publishers, 1991. Physical moves and the emotional adjustments they require are often painful and unsettling. They challenge our expectations, forcing us to come to terms with new realities. In this book, you'll follow the lives of four people whose idealism collided with the sobering realities of life, and you'll be encouraged by the surprising benefits their adjustments reveal.

His Sensitivity to a Boy's Death

Barber, Cyril J., and Sharalee Aspenleiter. *Through the Valley of Tears*. Old Tappan, N.J.: Fleming H. Revell Co., 1987. Sensitively written, this book will lead you through bereavement and give you wisdom and hope for the future.

His Confrontation with Idolatry

Smedes, Lewis B. *Love within Limits: Realizing Selfless Love in a Selfish World*. Grand Rapids, Mich.: William B. Eerdmans Publishing Co., 1978. God's "prove it" to Israel came in a blinding flash of fire. Today, God proves His reality through His family's practice of love. Smedes brings love down to where you live—realistically and practically.

His Prayer Life

Hybels, Bill. *Too Busy Not to Pray*. Downers Grove, Ill.: InterVarsity Press, 1988. If you want a powerful prayer life like Elijah's, then this book is for you. It will help you confront habits and thought patterns that keep you from slowing down long enough to nurture your relationship with God.

His Wilderness of Depression

Minirth, Frank B., and Paul D. Meier. *Happiness Is a Choice*. Grand Rapids, Mich.: Baker Book House, 1978. Abraham Lincoln once said, "Most people are about as happy as they choose to be."[1] Everyone is able to have inner peace and joy—if they follow the right path to obtain it. This book opens the road that leads away from dark moodiness to joy.

His Condemnation of Injustice

Colson, Charles, with Ellen Santilli Vaughn. *Kingdoms in Conflict*. New York, N.Y.: William Morrow; Grand Rapids, Mich.: Zondervan Publishing House; A Judith Markham Book, 1987. As power centers crumble and monetary systems fall apart, conflict and confusion increase. All earthly advice fails to fix the faltering systems, so what can we do? Colson asserts that the only

---

1. As quoted by Paul D. Meier in *Happiness Is a Choice*, p. 12.

solution is found in Christ, whose Word brings stability in a world of unrest.

His Counterattack against the Occult

Unger, Merrill F. *Demons in the World Today*. Wheaton, Ill.: Tyndale House Publishers, 1971. Fortune-telling, Ouija boards, demon possession, Satanism—these and many other mysteries of the occult world are examined thoroughly.

———. *The Mystery of Bishop Pike*. Wheaton, Ill.: Tyndale House Publishers, 1971. James A. Pike's life-altering experiences with the occult are examined through a scriptural grid in this enlightening book. The author demonstrates that Pike's contacts with the other side were actually with powerful and deceitful spirits who misled him about death, eternal life, and God.

His Heavenly Finish

Criswell, W. A., and Paige Patterson. *Heaven*. Wheaton, Ill.: Tyndale House Publishers, 1991. The authors open the window of Scripture to give us a glimpse of our eternal home with God. Far from the harp-strumming, "cloud-potato" images most of us have grown up with, they reveal heaven to be a place of purpose and adventure—equal to the grandeur of Elijah's majestic whirlwind and flaming chariot.

THE WANDERINGS OF ELIJAH
MID 9th CENTURY B.C.

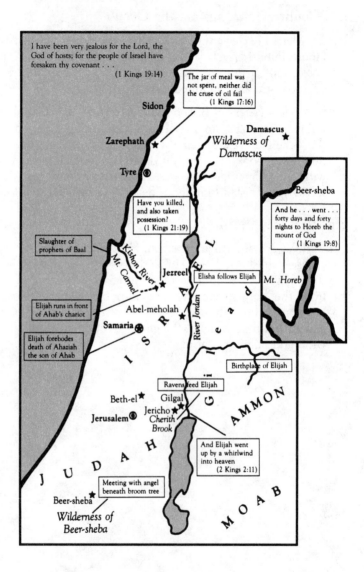

I have been very jealous for the Lord, the God of hosts; for the people of Israel have forsaken thy covenant . . .
(1 Kings 19:14)

The jar of meal was not spent, neither did the cruse of oil fail
(1 Kings 17:16)

Sidon

Damascus

Zarephath

Wilderness of Damascus

Tyre

Beer-sheba

Have you killed, and also taken possession?
(1 Kings 21:19)

And he . . . went . . . forty days and forty nights to Horeb the mount of God
(1 Kings 19:8)

Slaughter of prophets of Baal

Kishon River

Mt. Carmel

Jezreel

Elisha follows Elijah

Mt. Horeb

Elijah runs in front of Ahab's chariot

Abel-meholah

River Jordan

Samaria

Elijah forebodes death of Ahaziah the son of Ahab

ISRAEL

Gilead

Birthplace of Elijah

Ravens feed Elijah

AMMON

Beth-el

Gilgal

Jerusalem

Jericho
Cherith Brook

And Elijah went up by a whirlwind into heaven
(2 Kings 2:11)

JUDAH

Meeting with angel beneath broom tree

Beer-sheba

Wilderness of Beer-sheba

MOAB

Kings of Judah and Israel and the Preexilic Prophets

JUDAH

Kings	Dates	Years
Rehoboam	931–913	17
Abijah	913–911	3
Asa	911–870	41
Coregency with Jehoshaphat	873–870	(3)
Jehoshaphat	873–848	25
Coregency with Jehoram	853–848	(5)
Jehoram OBADIAH	848–841	8
Ahaziah	841	1
Queen Athaliah	841–835	6
Joash JOEL	835–796	40
Amaziah	796–767	29
Azariah's vice-regency under Amaziah	790–767	(23)
Azariah (Uzziah)	790–739	52
Coregency with Jotham	750–739	(11)
Jotham	750–735	16
Ahaz's vice-regency under Jotham	744–735	(9)
Coregency of Joham with Ahaz	735–732	4
Ahaz	732–715	16
Hezekiah's vice-regency under Ahaz	729–715	(14)
Hezekiah	715–686	29
Manasseh's vice-regency under Hezekiah	697–686	(11)
Manasseh NAHUM	697–642	55
Amon	642–640	2
Josiah ZEPHANIAH	640–609	31
Johoahaz	609	1/4
Jehoiakim HABAKKUK	609–598	11
Jehoiachin	598–597	1/4
Zedekiah	597–586	11

(Prophets in left margin: MICAH, ISAIAH, JEREMIAH)

ISRAEL

Kings	Dates	Years
Jeroboam 1	931–910	22
Nadab	910–909	2
Baasha	909–886	24
Elah	886–885	2
Zimri	885	7 days
Tibni	885–880	6
Overlapping reign with Omri	885–880	(6)
Omri	885–874	12
Ahab	874–853	22
Ahaziah	853–852	2
Jehoram (Joram)	852–841	12
Jehu	841–814	28
Jehoahaz	814–798	17
Jehoash (Joash)	798–782	16
Coregency with Jeroboam II	793–782	(11)
Jeroboam II JONAH AMOS	793–753	41
Zechariah	753–752	1/2
Shallum	752	1/12
Menahem	752–742	10
Overlapping reign with Pekah	752–742	(10)
Pekahiah	742–742	(2)
Overlapping reign with Pekah	742–740	(2)
Pekah	752–732	20
Hoshea	732–722	9

(Prophets in left margin: ELIJAH, ELISHA, HOSEA)

Chart adapted from John F. Walvoord and Roy B. Zuck, eds., *The Bible Knowledge Commentary* (Wheaton, Ill.: Scripture Press Publications, Victor Books, 1985), p. 513.

ORDERING INFORMATION

Cassette Tapes and Study Guide

This Bible study guide was designed to be used independently or in conjunction with the broadcast of Chuck Swindoll's taped messages on the topic listed below. If you would like to order cassette tapes or further copies of this study guide, please see the information given below and the Order Form provided on the last page of this guide.

THE LIFE AND TIMES OF ELIJAH

These biographical studies take us behind the scenes of a prophet's life. They do not hide the pain of obscurity, the lengthy ache of waiting, profound loneliness, misunderstanding, and depression. But you'll gain perspective as you are inspired by the miraculous power of God, His comfort to the hurting, and His rewards for those who trust Him. Elijah's experiences give new meaning to our lives!

			Calif.*	U.S.	B.C.*	Canada*
ELJ	CS	Cassette series, includes album cover	$31.64	$29.50	$45.01	$42.76
ELJ	1–5	Individual cassettes, include messages A and B	5.36	5.00	7.61	7.23
ELJ	SG	Study Guide	4.24	3.95	5.08	5.08

*These prices already include the following charges: for delivery in **California,** applicable sales tax; **Canada,** 7% GST and 7% postage and handling (on tapes only); **British Columbia,** 7% GST, 6% British Columbia sales tax (on tapes only), and 7% postage and handling (on tapes only). **The prices are subject to change without notice.**

ELJ	1-A:	*Standing Alone in the Gap*—1 Kings 16:29–17:1
	B:	*Boot Camp at Cherith*—1 Kings 17:1–7
ELJ	2-A:	*Advanced Training at Zarephath*—1 Kings 17:8–16
	B:	*A Miracle in the Home*—1 Kings 17:17–24
ELJ	3-A:	*The God Who Answers by Fire*—1 Kings 18:1–2, 17–40
	B:	*Kneeling on the Promises*—1 Kings 18:41–46
ELJ	4-A:	*Sure Cure for the Blues*—1 Kings 19:1–8, 21
	B:	*When God Says, "That's Enough!"*—1 Kings 21:1–29

ELJ   5-A: *Satanic Flies That Swarm Around Us*—
1 Kings 22:51–53; 2 Kings 1:1–18
  B: *A No-Death Contract*—2 Kings 2:1–14

How to Order by Mail

Simply mark on the order form whether you want the series or individual tapes. Mail the form with your payment to the appropriate address listed below. We will process your order as promptly as we can.

United States: Mail your order to the Listener Services Department at Insight for Living, Post Office Box 69000, Anaheim, California 92817-0900. If you wish your order to be shipped first-class for faster delivery, add 10 percent of the total order amount. Otherwise, please allow four to six weeks for delivery by fourth-class mail. We accept personal checks, money orders, Visa, or MasterCard in payment for materials. Unfortunately, we are unable to offer invoicing or COD orders.

Canada: Mail your order to Insight for Living Ministries, Post Office Box 2510, Vancouver, British Columbia V6B 3W7. Allow approximately four weeks for delivery. We accept personal checks, money orders, Visa, or MasterCard in payment for materials. Unfortunately, we are unable to offer invoicing or COD orders.

Australia, New Zealand, or Papua New Guinea: Mail your order to Insight for Living, Inc., GPO Box 2823 EE, Melbourne, Victoria 3001, Australia. Please allow six to ten weeks for delivery by surface mail. If you would like your order sent airmail, the delivery time may be reduced. Using the United States price as a base, add postage costs—surface or airmail—to the amount of your order. Please use the chart that follows to determine correct postage. Due to fluctuating currency rates, we can accept only personal checks made payable in U.S. funds, international money orders, Visa, or MasterCard in payment for materials.

Overseas: In other international locations, residents should mail their orders to our United States office. Please allow six to ten weeks for delivery by surface mail. If you would like your order sent airmail, the delivery time may be reduced. Using the United States price as a base, add postage costs—surface or airmail—to the amount of your order. Please use the chart that follows to determine correct postage. Due to fluctuating currency rates, we can accept only personal checks made payable in U.S. funds, international money orders, Visa, or MasterCard in payment for materials.

Type of Postage	Postage Cost
Surface	10% of total order
Airmail	25% of total order

For Faster Service, Order by Telephone or FAX

For Visa or MasterCard orders, you are welcome to use one of our toll-free numbers between the hours of 7:00 A.M. and 4:30 P.M., Pacific time, Monday through Friday, or our FAX numbers. The numbers to use from anywhere in the United States are 1-800-772-8888 or FAX (714) 575-5049. To order from Canada, call our Vancouver office using 1-800-663-7639 or FAX (604) 596-2975. Vancouver residents, call (604) 596-2910. Australian residents should phone (03) 872-4606. From other international locations, call our Listener Services Department at (714) 575-5000 in the United States.

Our Guarantee

Our cassettes are guaranteed for ninety days against faulty performance or breakage due to a defect in the tape. For best results, please be sure your tape recorder is in good operating condition and is cleaned regularly.

Note: To cover processing and handling, there is a $10 fee for *any* returned check.

Insight for Living Catalog

Request a free copy of the Insight for Living catalog of books, tapes, and study guides by calling 1-800-772-8888 in the United States or 1-800-663-7639 in Canada.

Order Form

ELJ CS represents the entire *The Life and Times of Elijah* series in a special album cover, while ELJ 1–5 are the individual tapes included in the series. ELJ SG represents this study guide, should you desire to order additional copies.

Item	Calif.*	Unit Price U.S.	B.C.*	Canada*	Quantity	Amount
ELJ CS	$31.64	$29.50	$45.01	$42.76		$
ELJ 1	5.36	5.00	7.61	7.23		
ELJ 2	5.36	5.00	7.61	7.23		
ELJ 3	5.36	5.00	7.61	7.23		
ELJ 4	5.36	5.00	7.61	7.23		
ELJ 5	5.36	5.00	7.61	7.23		
ELJ SG	4.24	3.95	5.08	5.08		

Subtotal	
Overseas Residents Pay U.S. price plus 10% surface postage or 25% airmail. Also, see "How to Order by Mail."	
U.S. First-Class Shipping For faster delivery, add 10% for postage and handling.	
Gift to Insight for Living Tax-deductible in the United States and Canada.	
Total Amount Due Please do not send cash.	$

If there is a balance: ☐ Apply it as a donation ☐ Please refund
*These prices already include applicable taxes and shipping costs.

Payment by: ☐ Check or money order made payable to Insight for Living or

☐ Credit card (circle one): Visa MasterCard Number _____

Expiration Date _____ Signature _____
We cannot process your credit card purchase without your signature.

Name _____

Address _____

City _____ State/Province _____

Zip/Postal Code _____ Country _____

Telephone ( ) _____ Radio Station ___ ___ ___ ___
If questions arise concerning your order, we may need to contact you.

Mail this order form to the Listener Services Department at one of these addresses:

Insight for Living, Post Office Box 69000, Anaheim, CA 92817-0900
Insight for Living Ministries, Post Office Box 2510, Vancouver, BC, Canada V6B 3W7
Insight for Living, Inc., GPO Box 2823 EE, Melbourne, VIC 3001, Australia